Choose the Right

A Year of Family Night Lessons to Help Your Children Choose the Right

KIMIKO CHRISTENSEN HAMMARI

CFI
An imprint of Cedar Fort, Inc.
Springville, Utah

For Mayumi, my little firecracker,
who I thought about while writing this book.
May you increase in wisdom and always
choose the right.

ISBN 13: 978-1-59955-941-4

Published by CFI, an imprint of Cedar Fort, Inc., 2373 W. 700 S., Springville, UT, 84663
Distributed by Cedar Fort, Inc., www.cedarfort.com

Cover design by Rebecca Jensen
Cover design © 2011 by Lyle Mortimer
Edited by Heidi Doxey

Printed in the United States of America

10 9 8 7 6 5 4 3 2 1

Printed on acid-free paper

Contents

July

August

September

October

November

December

Fun Food for FHE

How to Use This Book

This book provides a year's worth of family home evening lessons that teach your children how to increase their faith in Jesus Christ and make good choices. In order to get the most out of this manual and reinforce what your children are learning in Primary, teach the lessons in order. The lessons are divided into monthly themes and subdivided into weekly themes. Four lessons are provided for most months. However, in some months, there are only three. In those cases, use the extra week to review what you learned previously, or use it for those special Monday nights when family home evening takes on a different form (such as a school event that can't be missed or an extended family activity).

Each lesson is divided into the following sections:

Resources

Scriptures, Primary songs, hymns, and pictures from the Gospel Art Book.

(Note: The Gospel Art Book is available at www.lds.org. You can download and print pictures, or show the pictures to your children on the computer, if it is available during your lesson. You can order a copy of the Gospel Art Book at store.lds.org)

Lesson

A brief explanation of the theme with corresponding scriptures and discussion questions.

Activity

The activities are meant to reinforce what is taught in the lesson, so they may not be the games your family is used to playing. Most lessons include separate activities for younger children and older children. Generally the activities for younger children are for ages three to seven, and the older children, eight to eleven. However, don't use this guideline as a firm rule. Some younger children may be advanced for their age, and some older children may still enjoy the activities for younger children. You know your children best, so present the activities that you think they will enjoy.

Challenge

These challenges should be completed during the week before the next Monday. At the beginning of each family home evening, follow up with your children on the previous week's challenge. Discuss their success and help them with any problems or concerns. Each lesson includes a challenge card that should be printed from the CD. Each child should fill out a card and put it somewhere he will see it during the week so he can be reminded of what to work on. The challenge cards include a line where your child can sign his name and formally commit to the challenge. This method will help your child understand that writing down a goal makes it a more solid commitment.

CD-ROM

The CD has been provided for your convenience in printing handouts, challenge cards, and other lesson materials. This entire book is available on the CD and can be printed in color. It is recommended that you print out activities and challenge cards from the CD so you don't have to write in your book or cut it up. A "Read Me" file on the CD explains how to use it.

January

Agency Is the Gift to Choose for Ourselves

*Wherefore, men are free . . . to choose
liberty and eternal life, through the great
Mediator of all men*

(2 Nephi 2:27).

Agency is the gift to choose for ourselves.

Lesson

How would you feel if your parents made all your decisions for you? What if they never let you choose what flavor of ice cream you wanted or what game to play on family night? Because your parents love you, they want you to make choices for yourself. Even more important, Heavenly Father wants you to make your own decision whether or not you will follow Him. This is a special gift from Him called agency.

Because we have agency, we can choose whether we will keep the commandments. Of course Heavenly Father wants us to follow Him, but He loves us and will not force us to obey Him. If we choose not to follow Him, we cannot receive the blessings He has promised us. But it is still our choice. If we use our agency for good and keep the commandments, we will find great joy and receive eternal life.

Read and discuss Helaman 14:30.
+ What does it mean to act for yourself?
+ What will happen if you use your agency to disobey the commandments?

2

Activity

Younger Children: Let your children choose a game that they'd like to play. Explain that they are very blessed to have the freedom to choose.

Older Children: Have a scripture chase using scriptures that relate to agency. Look in the Topical Guide for ideas.

Challenge

Part of using agency is making good choices to bless others. This week be mindful of others when you make choices. For example, if your mom asks what you want for dinner, perhaps you could ask her to make something you know another member of your family would enjoy.

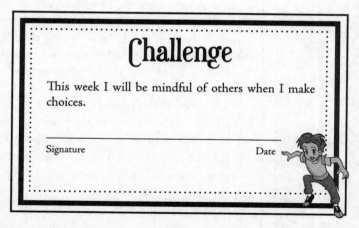

Challenge

This week I will be mindful of others when I make choices.

_____

Signature   Date

In the premortal life, I chose to follow God's plan.

Lesson

In the premortal life when we lived as God's spirit children, Heavenly Father presented a beautiful plan. We could come to earth and receive physical bodies like His. We could learn and grow, gain wisdom and knowledge, and eventually become like Him. He knew life on earth would be hard, so He wanted to send someone to help us choose the right. Lucifer said he would make sure everyone obeyed Heavenly Father. But in order to do this, he would take away our agency and force us to choose the right. Then he would glory in the fact that we all obeyed the commandments.

Jesus also volunteered to help us, but He had a better plan. He would love us and teach us how to choose the right. He knew we would still make mistakes, so He would be our Savior. Through the Atonement He would make it possible for us to repent. Then He would give the glory to Heavenly Father.

Lucifer's plan was not a righteous plan. He, along with those who chose to follow him, were cast out of heaven. The rest of us, who chose to follow Jesus, are here on earth. We are doing our best to choose the right and keep the commandments so we can live with Heavenly Father again someday.

Read and discuss Moses 1:39.
+ What is God's work and glory?
+ What does it mean "to bring to pass the immortality and eternal life of man"?

Activity

All Ages: Cut out several sets of footprints (see page 10 for a pattern), and lead them from one room to another. Place something appealing at the end of the footprints, such as a good book or a treat. Instruct your children to walk on the footprints and follow them to a prize. At the end, discuss how following God's plan leads to good things.

Challenge

As a family, memorize the song "I Will Follow God's Plan" (see *Children's Songbook*, 164).

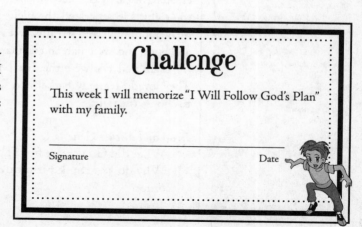

Challenge

This week I will memorize "I Will Follow God's Plan" with my family.

_____

Signature   Date

Jesus created the earth as a place where I can learn to choose the right.

Lesson

In the premortal world we were not able to learn and grow like we are here on earth. There was no evil, so we were not able to understand what it is like to choose the right. Heavenly Father knew that in order to develop faith and wisdom, we would need to come to earth so we could make choices.

Under the direction of Heavenly Father, Jesus Christ created the earth as a place where we can learn to choose the right. He separated the night from the day, then made mountains and streams, trees and plants, animals and bugs, and even man and woman.

Adam and Eve were the first people here on earth. They loved Heavenly Father and taught their children to choose the right.

Read and discuss Genesis 1.
- What did God create first? Last?
- Why do you think He created the earth in this order?

6

Activity

Younger Children: See page 8.
Older Children: See page 9.

Challenge

Heavenly Father and Jesus Christ created many beautiful things for us to enjoy. Each day this week, find one of Their creations that you are thankful for and write about it in your journal. It could be a flower, a beautiful sunset, an animal, or something similar.

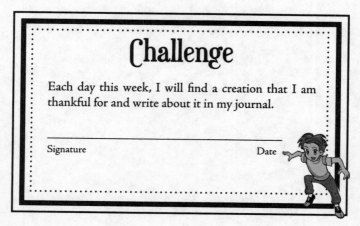

Challenge

Each day this week, I will find a creation that I am thankful for and write about it in my journal.

_____

Signature   Date

Jesus Created Many Beautiful Things

There are six of these flowers ❀ in the picture below. Can you find all of them?

Dominos

In each domino you will find two pictures of something Jesus created. Each picture matches the one in the domino next to it, except for two. Can you find them? *Solution on page 140.*

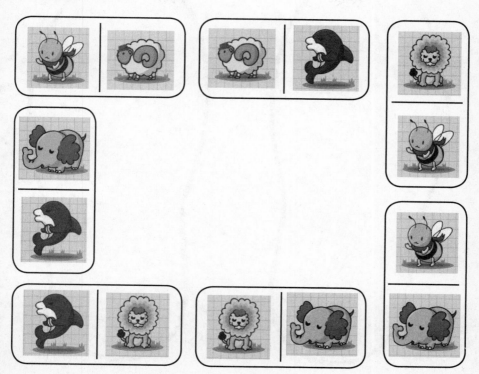

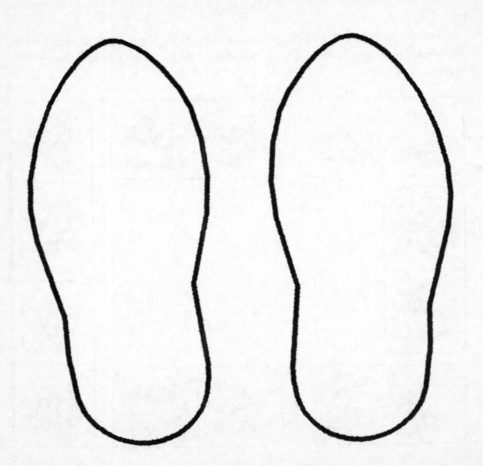

February

When We Choose the Right, We Are Blessed

*If ye do keep his commandments he doth bless you
and prosper you*
(Mosiah 2:22).

Week 1

Noah was blessed for choosing the right.

Resources

(Select one from each category.)

Children's Songbook
+ Dare to Do Right (158)
+ Choose the Right Way (160)

Hymn
+ Come, Listen to a Prophet's Voice (21)
+ We Listen to a Prophet's Voice (22)

Gospel Art Book
+ Building the Ark (7)
+ Noah and the Ark with Animals (8)

Scriptures
+ Hebrews 11:7
+ 2 Peter 2:5

Lesson

A long time ago, in Old Testament times, the people in the world were very wicked. Heavenly Father was sad that they did not choose the right. He told his prophet Noah to preach repentance to them, but no one except Noah's family would listen.

Because the world was so wicked, God decided to send a giant flood that would destroy the wicked. But Noah was righteous and God wanted to save him. He commanded Noah to build an ark, a giant boat that would protect him and his family from the flood. Noah took his family and two animals of each kind onto the ark. Even though it rained for forty days and forty nights, Noah and his family were protected because they chose the right.

Read and discuss Genesis 6:12–14.
+ What had happened to the earth?
+ Why did God command Noah to build an ark?

Activity

Younger Children: See page 14.

Older Children: Print the ark on page 15 from the resource CD (enlarge it if possible). Tape the ark to the wall or put it on the refrigerator. Give each family member a small piece of paper and have them write down something they can do to choose the right. Then, using the ark and the strips of paper, play a version of Pin the Tail on the Donkey. Afterward, tape or glue all the strips of paper on the ark. Leave it on the wall or on the refrigerator all week as a reminder that we are blessed when we choose the right.

Challenge

Each day we make many small choices, such as choosing to be kind to others or choosing to do our chores. Making small choices helps us have the strength to choose the right when we are faced with bigger choices. Each night this week during dinner, tell your family about one good choice you made that day.

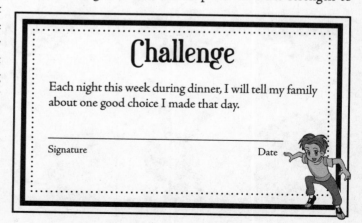

Challenge

Each night this week during dinner, I will tell my family about one good choice I made that day.

_____

Signature   Date

Two of Each Kind

Noah took two animals of each kind on the ark. Draw a line from the male animal to the matching female animal.

MALE   FEMALE

Week 2

Jesus's disciples were blessed by choosing the right.

Resources

(Select one from each category.)

Children's Songbook
- I'm Trying to Be Like Jesus (78)
- Teach Me to Walk in the Light (177)

Hymn
- God Speed the Right (106)
- I Believe in Christ (134)

Gospel Art Book
- Christ in the Home of Mary and Martha (45)

Scriptures
- Joshua 24:15
- 2 Nephi 10:23

Lesson

Read and discuss the story of Mary and Martha in Luke 10:38–42.

- What was Mary focused on? What was Martha focused on?
- What did Jesus say Mary had chosen?
- What are some of the things we sometimes worry about when we should focus on Jesus's teachings?

Activity

Younger Children: Color the picture on page 18.

Older Children: Read the following statements to your children. Have them decide if the child is choosing the right. If so, your children should draw a smile on the corresponding face on page 19. If the child is not choosing the right, your children should draw a frown.

1. Sara was quiet during family home evening and paid attention to the lesson.

2. Benny took out the trash without being asked.
3. TJ went to Primary instead of to a soccer game.
4. Lisa did not go straight home after school, even though her mother asked her to.
5. Sean lied to his parents when they asked him if he hit his younger brother.
6. Mayumi received ten dollars for her birthday and paid one dollar in tithing.

Challenge

In the story of Mary and Martha, Mary chose to focus on Jesus and His teachings, while Martha felt it was important to focus on things like taking care of the house. Both are important, but listening to Jesus is more important. This week make a choice to follow Jesus before taking care of other things. For example, your family could read the scriptures first thing in the morning. Or, you could decide to read the scriptures or sing Primary songs instead of watching TV.

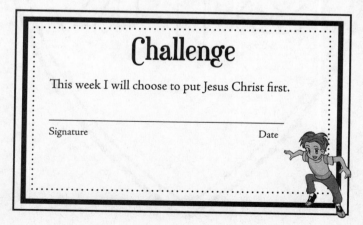

Challenge

This week I will choose to put Jesus Christ first.

_____

Signature   Date

Did I Choose the Right?

Listen to the stories your parents tell you about each child. Draw a smile on the child's face if he chose the right and a frown if he didn't.

Week 3

Nephi was blessed for choosing the right.

Lesson

Nephi and his family had to flee Jerusalem because the people there were wicked. Heavenly Father said He would destroy Jerusalem, but He wanted to protect Nephi and his family because they were righteous. God commanded them to go into the wilderness and search for a land that He had prepared for them. This is called the promised land.

Nephi and his family obeyed. They did not know where they were going but had faith that God would lead them. God gave them the Liahona, which was like a compass or GPS. Nephi described it as a ball of "curious workmanship" that pointed them in the right direction. But it only worked when they were choosing the right. If the family argued or made other wrong choices, the Liahona would not work until they repented.

Eventually Nephi and his family made it to the promised land. They were very happy and thanked God for protecting them. God promised them that as long as they kept the commandments, they would always prosper in the land.

Read and discuss 1 Nephi 2:20.
- What did the Lord promise Nephi?
- What does the promised land symbolize in this verse?

Activity

All Ages, Option 1: If your family has a GPS, go for a ride in the car and use the GPS to get to your destination. Each time the GPS gives you a direction, point out to your children that the GPS is giving directions, just like the Liahona did for Nephi's family. Purposely make a couple wrong turns to show your children how the GPS has to recalculate. Explain that the Liahona only worked when Nephi and his family were righteous. When they sinned, they had to repent before the Liahona would work again.

All Ages, Option 2: Play a game of charades. Act out different scenes from Nephi's life in which he chose the right.

Challenge

Each day this week, think about your actions and what you can do to choose the right.

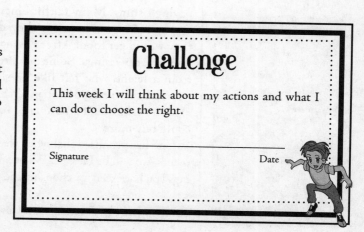

Challenge

This week I will think about my actions and what I can do to choose the right.

_____

Signature   Date

Week 4

Church members today are blessed for choosing the right.

Resources

(Select one from each category.)

Children's Songbook
* I Want to Live the Gospel (148)
* Stand for the Right (159)

Hymn
* Let Us All Press On (243)
* Who's on the Lord's Side? (260)

Gospel Art Book
* Family Prayer (112)
* Payment of Tithing (113)

Scriptures
* Joshua 24:15
* Alma 30:8

Lesson

Each time we choose the right, Heavenly Father blesses us. Sometimes we are able to see the blessings. Sometimes the blessings come as peace that we did the right thing. No matter how we are blessed, we should remember that Heavenly Father is happy when we choose the right.

Some members of the Church do not have a lot of money. They have to choose between buying food or paying tithing. Many faithful members have chosen to pay tithing, even when they didn't know where they would get food. After paying tithing, they have seen great blessings. Some people have received food from a friend who felt like he should share. Some people have received money. Others have been able able to make small amounts of food last until they could buy more.

God has promised that when we keep the commandments, we will be blessed. What are some of the blessings you have seen for choosing the right?

Read and discuss Doctrine and Covenants 130:20–22.

- How do we receive blessings?
- What are some of the blessings you have seen for choosing the right?

Activity

Younger Children: Make a creation that reminds you of something you have been blessed with. You can draw or paint a picture, model something out of Play-Doh, or do something similar.

Older Children: Print page 24 from the resource CD. (If possible, enlarge it.) Cut out the tree trunk and the leaves separately. Hang the tree on the wall. Ask your children to think of blessings they have received from choosing the right, and write one blessing on each leaf. Take turns putting the leaves on the tree.

Challenge

If you have a CTR ring, wear it each day this week to remind yourself to choose the right. If you don't have a CTR ring, wear a different ring or another piece of jewelry. Every time you see it, remind yourself to choose the right.

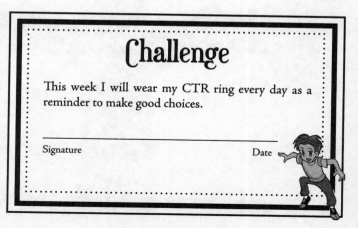

Challenge

This week I will wear my CTR ring every day as a reminder to make good choices.

_____
Signature   Date

March

Living Prophets Teach Me to Choose the Right

*O, remember, my son, and learn wisdom
in thy youth; yea, learn in thy youth to keep
the commandments of God*
(Alma 37:35).

Week 1

God speaks through living prophets.

Lesson

A couple weeks ago, we learned about the prophet Noah and how God protected him from the flood that destroyed the earth. Did you know that we have a prophet on the earth today? He is just as important and powerful as Noah. He holds the priesthood of God and has been called to speak the will of God. If Heavenly Father has a message for us, He talks to the prophet, who then speaks to us.

The prophet today is Thomas S. Monson. *[Show a picture of him.]* He loves Heavenly Father and Jesus very much, and he loves you and me, even though he has never met us. He is a righteous man who prays to know what to teach us. He testifies of Jesus Christ, warns us of danger, and helps us choose the right. He has promised to never lead us astray. We are very blessed to have a prophet on the earth today.

Read and discuss Doctrine and Covenants 1:38.
+ How are the Lord's voice and the prophet's voice the same?
+ What counsel has the prophet given us recently?

26

Activity

All Ages: Watch a conference talk by President Monson. Listen for ways that he tells us we can choose the right.

Challenge

President Monson is a great example of how to live. What are some of his traits that you admire? His love for others? The way he constantly serves? His commitment to Jesus Christ? Pick one of those traits and work on it this week.

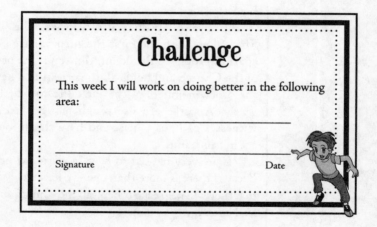

Challenge

This week I will work on doing better in the following area:

_____

_____

Signature   Date

The First Presidency and the Twelve Apostles are prophets.

Lesson

Last week we learned about the prophet, Thomas S. Monson. Did you know that he has two counselors to help him, just like the bishop has two counselors? The prophet and his counselors are called the First Presidency.

The Twelve Apostles also help lead the Church. They, along with the First Presidency, have been set apart as prophets. President Monson is the president of the Church and holds all the priesthood keys. But the other members of the First Presidency and the Twelve Apostles are also prophets. They are special witnesses of Jesus Christ and have the authority to act in His name.

We are very blessed to have modern-day prophets. Because there is more than one, we have the assurance that they will help each other lead the Church and never lead us astray.

Read and discuss Doctrine and Covenants 18:26–27.
+ Who are the Twelve Apostles?
+ How are they disciples of Jesus Christ?

28

Activity

Younger Children: See page 30.
Older Children: See page 31.

Challenge

Learn all the names of the First Presidency and Twelve Apostles.

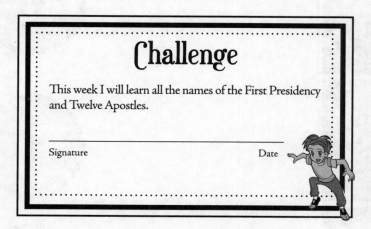

Challenge

This week I will learn all the names of the First Presidency and Twelve Apostles.

_____

Signature   Date

The First Presidency

Draw a line from the picture of the member of the First Presidency to his calling. P=prophet, 1=1st counselor, and 2=2nd counselor.

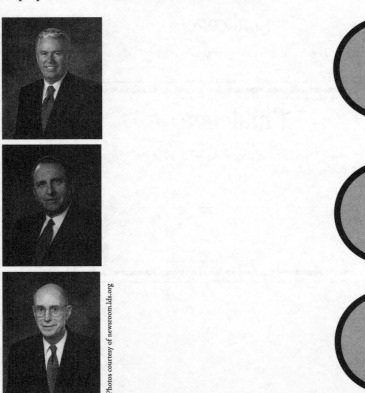

Photos courtesy of newsroom.lds.org

Word Search

Find the last names of the First Presidency and Twelve Apostles in the word search. Words appear forward, backward, horizontally, and vertically. *Solution on page 140.*

MONSON

EYRING

UCHTDORF

PACKER

PERRY

NELSON

OAKS

BALLARD

SCOTT

HALES

HOLLAND

BEDNAR

COOK

CHRISTOFFERSON

ANDERSEN

K	Z	W	O	S	I	D	H	B	H	I	P	M	X	E	B	A	W
E	Y	R	I	N	G	R	A	E	D	L	B	E	D	N	A	R	P
N	U	C	I	B	L	A	Q	K	Z	E	K	C	P	H	S	W	E
C	Z	U	Z	H	Y	L	W	T	I	X	Z	B	O	K	T	R	A
G	S	T	Q	J	B	L	M	O	N	S	O	N	A	D	J	S	V
U	N	I	B	O	R	A	I	H	G	S	W	O	S	J	A	H	W
C	W	S	O	W	Y	B	U	S	L	I	Z	M	A	R	I	J	D
H	N	O	S	R	E	F	F	O	T	S	I	R	H	C	P	C	N
T	T	K	R	J	O	E	M	Y	K	A	N	P	U	V	Q	F	B
D	K	Y	W	X	D	D	D	K	N	P	E	E	D	U	Q	E	I
O	D	B	R	R	T	Q	O	D	A	R	P	H	T	L	O	U	E
R	M	U	N	P	L	M	E	C	R	U	C	O	R	E	K	Q	X
F	G	E	B	O	O	R	K	Y	B	B	S	L	P	A	Y	T	H
F	W	C	M	C	S	E	V	A	D	G	C	L	L	V	W	A	I
B	P	P	O	E	R	L	I	U	V	F	O	A	A	O	L	Y	N
P	Z	G	N	O	F	K	E	B	G	O	T	N	R	E	A	C	P
Z	C	F	U	B	K	O	I	N	A	L	T	D	S	Y	Z	W	R

Week 3

God's prophets and apostles speak to us in general conference.

Lesson

April and October are important months. On the first weekend of these months, we get to listen to the prophets and apostles speak to us in general conference. They pray beforehand to know what Heavenly Father wants them to say. Because of this, they are speaking for Heavenly Father.

General conference takes place in Salt Lake City at the Conference Center on Temple Square. Thousands of people go there to listen to the prophets and apostles. But there are many people in the world, and not everyone can go to Salt Lake City. Those of us who don't attend general conference in person can watch it on television or on the Internet. We can even listen to it on the radio. No matter where we live, we can listen to the prophets and apostles speak, and we can hear the word of God.

Read and discuss Amos 3:7.
+ What are some of the things the prophet and apostles have taught recently in general conference?
+ How can we hear conference talks if we can't go to Salt Lake City?

Activity

All Ages: Make a general conference journal. Decorate a notebook or staple several pieces of paper together and make a cover with construction paper. Use this journal during general conference to write down the names of the speakers and three things that they mention in their talks. You can also draw pictures that help you remember their talks.

Challenge

To get ready for general conference, read or watch a recent conference talk of your choice with your family.

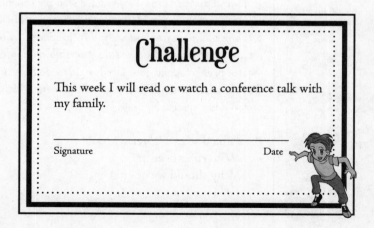

Challenge

This week I will read or watch a conference talk with my family.

_____   _____
Signature   Date

Week 4

I am blessed when I choose to follow the prophet.

Lesson

[Personalize this lesson to your family's specific experiences with following the prophet. Discuss with your children some of the prophets' counsel that your family has obeyed and how it has blessed your family. For example, maybe you have used your food storage recently due to financial difficulties or natural disasters; maybe you have seen the benefits from regular scripture study. Holding family home evening is also a commandment from modern-day prophets. Whatever you decide to focus on, make sure your children understand that the prophet spoke, your family made a decision to follow the counsel/commandment, and you have been blessed. Be sure to name specific blessings.]

Read and discuss Hebrews 13:17.

+ Who rules over us?
+ Why should we obey them?

Activity

Younger Children: Play a game of Simon Says. Pick a member of the family to be Simon and give the rest of the family directions. Explain how following Simon relates to following the prophet.

Older Children: See page 36.

Challenge

Watch all four sessions of general conference with your family. Use the conference journal you created last week to take notes or draw pictures that remind you of the talks.

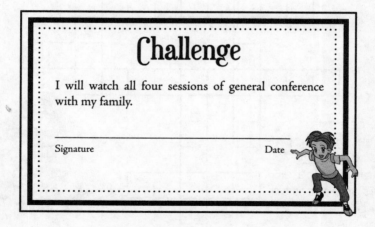

Challenge

I will watch all four sessions of general conference with my family.

_____

Signature   Date

Crossword Puzzle
COUNSEL FROM THE PROPHET

ACROSS

2. Obey the Word of _____.
4. Plant a _____.
5. Hold _____ home evening.
7. Girls should wear only ____ earring.
8. Study the _____.
10. We should pray _____.

DOWN

1. Have at least a three-month supply of food _____.
3. Do not have these types of pictures on your bodies.
6. Watch clean _____.
9. Pay your _____.

36

April

Jesus Christ Teaches Me to Choose the Right

For I have given you an example,
that ye should do as I have done to you
(John 13:15).

Jesus Christ is the perfect example for me.

Lesson

Who do you admire? Your parents? Your friends? A famous person? All around us we have good and bad examples. It's great if you have someone to look up to who chooses the right. But sometimes the people we look up to make wrong choices and don't want to repent.

There's one person we can always count on to set a good example: Jesus Christ. He is perfect, and He will never lead us astray. Sometimes it's hard to choose the right. But whenever we face a tough decision, we can ask ourselves, "What would Jesus do?"

Jesus always chose the right. Even though He was tempted at times, He never sinned. He did hard things because He knew His actions would bless others. When He was in the Garden of Gethsemane, He experienced so much pain that He bled from every pore. The Atonement was very difficult to perform, and He was tempted to give up. In the book of Matthew we are told that He asked Heavenly Father to take the pain away. But then, knowing that He had to continue, He said, "Nevertheless not as I will, but as thou wilt" (26:39). Jesus knew that if He gave up, none of us would be able to repent of our sins. If that happened, none of us could to return to Heavenly Father. He loved us so much that He endured the pain in order to help every person in this world.

Heavenly Father asks us to do hard things. But He will always give us the strength to do them. If we remember the example of Jesus Christ, it will be much easier to choose the right.

Read and discuss 3 Nephi 27:27.
+   What type of person should we be?
+   How can we follow Jesus Christ's example?

Activity

Younger Children: As a family, sing several rounds of "Do As I'm Doing." Choose someone to be the leader and perform actions such as rolling your arms, nodding your head, clapping, or anything else you find appropriate. Afterward remind your children how important it is to have good examples in our lives, especially that of Jesus Christ.
Older Children: See page 40.

Challenge

Do something this week that you know is right, even if you don't feel like it. For example, if your parents ask you to do the dishes, willingly agree. (See page 41 for the challenge card.)

Hangman

Use some of the phrases below (or create your own) to play Hangman with your family. Each completed puzzle will tell your family what you can do to follow Jesus Christ's example. If possible, use a chalkboard or dry erase board so everyone can see. A large piece of paper will also work.

BE KIND TO OTHERS

GO TO CHURCH

READ THE SCRIPTURES

PRAY OFTEN

DO MISSIONARY WORK

OBEY PARENTS

OBEY CHURCH LEADERS

PAY TITHING

HELP THE POOR

VOLUNTEER OUR TIME

RESPECT OTHERS

BE BAPTIZED BY IMMERSION

GO TO THE TEMPLE

ATTEND PRIMARY ACTIVITIES

RESPECT GOD'S CREATIONS

HOLD FAMILY HOME EVENING

OBEY THE WORD OF WISDOM

LISTEN TO GOOD MUSIC

WATCH GOOD MOVIES

Challenge

This week I will do something that I know is right, even if I don't feel like doing it. I will obey without complaining.

_____

Signature   Date

Weeks 2&3

Jesus Christ taught me the right way to live.

Resources

(Select one from each category.)

Children's Songbook
+ I Believe in Being Honest (149)
+ I Pledge Myself to Love the Right (161)

Hymn
+ Come unto Him (114)
+ Come, Follow Me (116)

Gospel Art Book
+ The Sermon on the Mount (39)
+ Jesus Washing the Feet of the Apostles (55)

Scriptures
+ 1 Peter 2:21
+ 3 Nephi 12:48

Lesson

When Jesus Christ was on the earth, He taught His gospel and the right way to live. He taught that we should love our neighbor, be kind to everyone, and obey the commandments. But Jesus didn't just teach with words. He taught us by example.

One day Jesus was very tired. A group of people came to Him and wanted Him to bless their children. Knowing Jesus was tired, His Apostles wanted to turn the people away. But Jesus responded, "Suffer the little children to come unto me" (Mark 10:14). This is one way Jesus taught us to put others before ourselves.

During the Last Supper, Jesus washed His apostles' feet. That was something a servant would normally do for his master. But Jesus, being the Master of us all, was humble and performed this great act of service for His apostles.

Jesus spent His life serving others. He taught that service is the only way to come unto Him. In Matthew 25:40 we read, "Verily I say unto you, Inasmuch as ye have done it unto one of the least of these my brethren, ye have done it unto me."

42

Read and discuss 2 Nephi 31:16.

- ◆ Whom do we need to follow to be saved?
- ◆ How can we endure to the end?

Activity

All Ages: Jesus often taught in parables. As a family, read one of the parables and discuss its meaning. Be sure that each child understands how it relates to him. Then make a collage with pictures that represent what Jesus taught in the parable. Hang it in the dining room or another place where each family member will see it often.

Challenge

Jesus taught many wonderful truths in the Sermon on the Mount. Read it during family scripture study this week and discuss how following these teachings can help you and your family choose the right.

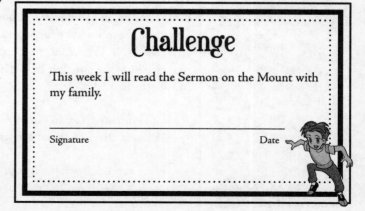

Challenge

This week I will read the Sermon on the Mount with my family.

_____

Signature   Date

I feel my Savior's love when I try to be like Jesus Christ.

Resources

(Select one from each category.)

Children's Songbook
+ I Feel My Savior's Love (74)
+ Love One Another (136)

Hymn
+ Our Savior's Love (113)
+ Lord, I Would Follow Thee (220)

Gospel Art Book
+ Christ Raising the Daughter of Jairus (41)
+ The Good Samaritan (44)

Scriptures
+ 2 Nephi 26:30
+ Moroni 7:45–48.

Lesson

How do you feel when you choose the right? It is impossible to do something good and feel bad about it. When we make good choices, we feel happy and peaceful. The Holy Ghost tells us that what we did was good and helps us feel close to Jesus Christ.

It has been said that we develop love for others by serving them. Have you felt this? How do you feel when you help your parents around the house, or when you help your brother or sister with a chore? When we serve others, we begin to understand how Jesus Christ feels about us. We feel charity for others.

In the New Testament, the Apostle Paul explained that charity is the pure love of Christ. Let's read about it in 1 Corinthians 13.

Read and discuss 1 Corinthians 13:1–8.

+ What is charity? What are some of its characteristics?
+ How can we develop charity? (See Moroni 7:48).

44

Activity

All Ages: Do a service project together as a family. See page 46 for ideas.

Challenge

Think about times when you chose the right. How did you feel? Write about one of these experiences in your journal. How did that experience help you feel your Savior's love?

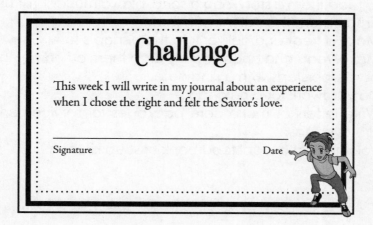

Challenge

This week I will write in my journal about an experience when I chose the right and felt the Savior's love.

_____

Signature   Date

Service Project Ideas

1. Take a meal to someone who has had surgery or recently had a baby.
2. Wash someone's car.
3. Write letters to missionaries or people in the ward who are ill or having a hard time.
4. Pick up trash around your neighborhood or a building that is important to you (school, church, and so on).
5. Go to a rest home and visit the residents. You may also want to read them a story, sing a song, play a musical instrument, or share another talent with them.
6. Make a treat and deliver it to the bishop's family.
7. Make treats and anonymously drop them off on your neighbors' doorsteps with a kind note.
8. Do yardwork for a neighbor.
9. Write letters or make care packages for servicemen who are overseas.
10. Volunteer at a local food bank or soup kitchen.

May

I Choose the Right When I Am Baptized and Confirmed a Member of the Church

Repent, and be baptized every one of you in the name of Jesus Christ for the remission of sins, and ye shall receive the gift of the Holy Ghost

(Acts 2:38).

As I repent, I can be forgiven.

Resources

(Select one from each category.)

Children's Songbook
+ Repentance (98)
+ The Fourth Article of Faith (124)

Hymn
+ Prayer Is the Soul's Sincere Desire (145)
+ Father in Heaven, We Do Believe (180)

Gospel Art Book
+ The Crucifixion (57)
+ The Lost Lamb (64)

Scriptures
+ Psalm 38:18
+ Alma 34:33

Lesson

The only way to return to Heavenly Father is to follow Jesus Christ and keep all the commandments. But when He sent us to earth, Heavenly Father knew we would not always choose the right. He provided a Savior for us so we can repent of our sins and be forgiven. Because Jesus Christ died for us, we can be washed clean from our sins.

We must take certain steps to be forgiven. First, we admit that we made a mistake and feel godly sorrow for our sins. That means we feel sad that we sinned and wish we hadn't done it. There is a difference between feeling godly sorrow and feeling sorrow because we have to face the consequences of our sins.

Second, we forsake, or stop, our sins. If we have lied, we must stop lying. If we have been unkind to someone, we must stop being unkind.

Third, we confess our sins to Heavenly Father and anyone else that we want to forgive us. If we called someone a bad name, we must confess that sin to both Heavenly Father and the person we hurt.

Fourth, we make restitution. That means we try to correct the wrong act. If we have stolen something, we return the item to the owner or find a way to pay for it.

Fifth, we forgive others. God cannot forgive us if we don't forgive others.

Finally, we keep the commandments of God. We are not fully repentant if we don't continue doing our best to choose the right.

Repentance can be hard, but we will find great joy in giving up our sins and following Jesus Christ.

Read and discuss Isaiah 1:18.
+ What are scarlet and crimson?
+ How does the turning of these colors to white represent repentance?

Activity

Younger Children: Give each child a piece of paper and a pencil with a good eraser. Tell them to draw or write anything they want on the paper. Then show them how to erase the pictures or words. Explain how repentance is like an eraser that removes our sins.

Older Children: See page 50.

Challenge

We should repent often, even daily if necessary. This week at the end of each day, think about what you have done that day. If you have done something you shouldn't have, repent now. Repentance only gets harder the longer we wait. (See page 51 for challenge card.)

Repentance Word Scramble

Unscramble the words below. When you are finished, see if you can remember how these words were used in this week's lesson. **Solution on page 140.**

1. TAMID

2. WORRSO

3. RASFEOK

4. FENSOSC

5. ERIITTOSTUN

6. RFOVGIE

7. YOBE

8. DUREND OT HET DEN

Repentance isn't easy, but it brings great joy.

Challenge

This week at the end of each day, I will think about what I did that day and repent of any sins.

_____

Signature   Date

Week 2

When I am baptized and confirmed, I am following Jesus's example.

Resources

(Select one from each category.)

Children's Songbook
- When Jesus Christ Was Baptized (102)
- The Holy Ghost (105)

Hymn
- Lead Me into Life Eternal (45)
- Lord, Accept into Thy Kingdom (236)

Gospel Art Book
- John Baptizes Jesus (35)
- Girl Being Baptized (104)
- The Gift of the Holy Ghost (105)

Scriptures
- Acts 2:38
- 3 Nephi 12:2

Lesson

In the New Testament we can read about John the Baptist, who held the priesthood and baptized many people. One day Jesus went to John and asked to be baptized. John felt very unworthy to baptize the Savior. He didn't understand why a perfect person needed to be baptized. Jesus told John that He needed to be baptized to fulfill all righteousness. John baptized Jesus in the Jordan River. Afterward, the Holy Ghost descended upon Him in the form of a dove.

Jesus loves Heavenly Father. He wanted to keep all of the commandments. Being baptized and confirmed a member of the Church is a commandment. Jesus Christ set a great example for us.

As soon as you turn eight, you can be baptized and confirmed if you are worthy. Baptism is a very important step that we must take to return to Heavenly Father. When we are baptized, we enter a symbolic gate that leads to Heavenly Father.

Read and discuss our baptismal covenants in Mosiah 18:8–10.

- What do we promise Heavenly Father when we are baptized?
- What does Heavenly Father promise to do for us?

Activity

Younger Children: Color the picture on page 57.
Older Children: Play Baptism Card Match found on the next three pages. Match the covenants with the person making the covenant. For example, the card "serve others and Jesus Christ" matches with the card that says "My Covenant." (Parents: Print the cards from the resource CD.)

Challenge

If you have been baptized, write about your experience in your journal. What do you remember about that special day? Who baptized you? Who came to witness it? How did you feel? If you have not been baptized, write about (or draw a picture of) what you are looking forward to most about your baptism and what you can do to prepare for it.

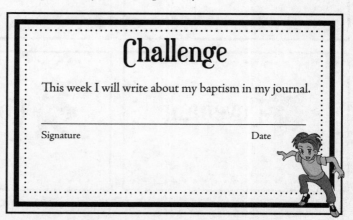

Challenge

This week I will write about my baptism in my journal.

_____
Signature   Date

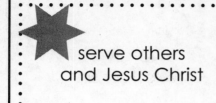
serve others
and Jesus Christ

repent of
our sins

keep the
commandments

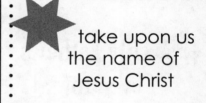
take upon us
the name of
Jesus Christ

always
remember Jesus

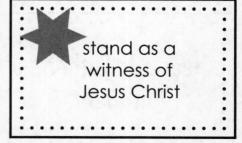
stand as a
witness of
Jesus Christ

Heavenly Father's Covenant	forgive us of our sins
Heavenly Father's Covenant	give us the gift of the Holy Ghost
Heavenly Father's Covenant	give us eternal life

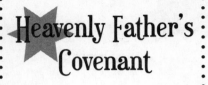

When I am baptized, I promise to be kind to others.

The Holy Ghost can help me.

Lesson

Heavenly Father has not left us alone here on earth. The Holy Ghost, the third member of the Godhead, helps us in many ways. He helps us know if something is true. He warns us of danger. He helps us remember things. He teaches us truth. He guides us and helps us understand how God answers our prayers. He comforts us and helps us feel loved when we are sad.

We cannot see the Holy Ghost, but we can feel His influence. Some people say they hear a still, small voice when the Holy Ghost speaks to them. Other people feel good and say that things just make sense in their minds. No matter how the Holy Ghost speaks to us, we all feel similar things when the Holy Ghost is present. We feel peace and joy. Some people have a warm feeling in their heart. When have you felt the Holy Ghost?

Read and discuss Galatians 5:22–23.
+ What is the fruit of the Spirit?
+ When have you experienced these feelings?

58

Activity

Younger Children: Tell your children you have something very important to tell them and to listen carefully. Then turn on some loud music while you give them the message. Make sure the music is loud enough that they can't hear you. Then turn the music off and ask your children what you just told them. Explain that we must listen very carefully in order to hear the Holy Ghost, and that when we have distractions it is difficult to discern what He is trying to tell us.

Older Children: Before family home evening begins, choose a question to ask your children. (This can be any question, ranging from gospel topics to everyday subjects.) Hide the answer to the question somewhere in the room (a sign on the door, a bookmark in the scriptures, or someone mouthing the answer), and tell your children to look for it. Explain that we have to listen very carefully to the still, small voice and that sometimes the answers to our prayers are found in unexpected places.

Challenge

This week pay attention to times when you feel the Holy Ghost. Then write about those experiences in your journal.

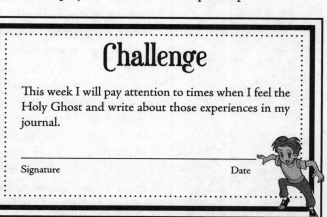

Challenge

This week I will pay attention to times when I feel the Holy Ghost and write about those experiences in my journal.

_____   _____
Signature   Date

Week 4

Resources

(Select one from each category.)

Children's Songbook
- The Sacrament (72)
- Before I Take the Sacrament (73)

Hymn
- As Now We Take the Sacrament (169)
- While of These Emblems We Partake (173)

Gospel Art Book
- Blessing the Sacrament (107)
- Passing the Sacrament (108)

Scriptures
- John 6:54
- D&C 20:75

When I take the sacrament I renew my baptismal covenants.

Lesson

When we are baptized, we promise to follow Jesus Christ. As much as we want to follow Him, we still sin afterward. Fortunately, we can always repent of our sins. We should repent often, even daily if necessary.

Each Sunday we renew our baptismal covenants when we take the sacrament. Although we are baptized only once, we can recommit (promise again) each week to choose the right.

You have probably noticed that the chapel is very quiet during the sacrament. That is because the sacrament is a sacred ordinance. We need to focus our thoughts on Jesus and think about how we can better follow Him. And we need to be quiet so that those around us can do the same.

During the sacrament, some people read from the hymn book or from their scriptures. Others like to just think about what Jesus Christ means to them. Whatever you choose to do, make sure that your thoughts are focused on Jesus and His sacrifice for us. Think about what you can do that week to be a better disciple of Jesus Christ.

Read and discuss the sacrament prayers in Doctrine and Covenants 20:77, 79.
+ What covenants do we renew when we take the sacrament?
+ What does God promise us if we keep our covenants?

Activity

Younger Children: Go on a picture scavenger hunt. Look through the *Friend* magazine, the *Gospel Art Book*, and other publications for pictures of people keeping their baptismal covenants. Find at least five pictures.
Older Children: See page 62.

Challenge

Be reverent during the sacrament next week. Think about Jesus, say a silent prayer, read your scriptures, or do something else that helps you remember the purpose of the sacrament.

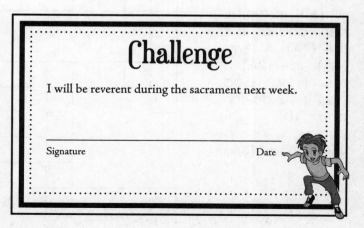

Challenge

I will be reverent during the sacrament next week.

_____

Signature   Date

Crossword Puzzle

MORMON 9:29

Complete the crossword puzzle by filling in the missing words from the verse below. For example, 2A in the verse below is the missing word that goes in 2 across, 1D is 1 down, and so forth. *Solution on page 140.*

See that ye are not **(4A)** unworthily; see that ye partake not of the **(2D)** of Christ **(5A)**; but see that ye do all **(6D)** in worthiness, and do it in the **(7A)** of Jesus **(8A)**, the **(2A)** of the living God; and if ye do this, and **(1D)** to the end, ye will in nowise be cast **(3A)**.

June

I Choose the Right by Living Gospel Principles

I will go and do the things which the Lord hath commanded, for I know that the Lord giveth no commandments unto the children of men, save he shall prepare a way for them that they may accomplish the thing which he commandeth them

(1 Nephi 3:7).

Week 1

I pray to Heavenly Father for strength to do what is right.

Lesson

Sylvia had many friends at school. One day her teacher told her that a new girl in their class didn't have anyone to play with at recess. She asked Sylvia to be her friend and play with her.

All morning, Sylvia was very afraid of what her friends would think at recess. The new girl was very shy. She didn't look like Sylvia's friends, and she dressed differently. Sylvia was afraid her friends would tease her for asking the new girl to play with them.

Suddenly Sylvia remembered something her parents had taught her. She could pray anytime, anywhere, and Heavenly Father would help her choose the right. When there was a quiet moment in the classroom, Sylvia said a prayer in her heart and asked Heavenly Father for strength. She also prayed that her friends would accept the new girl.

When the bell rang and the class went outside for recess, Sylvia saw all of her friends gathering together. Then she looked behind her and saw the new girl standing alone against the wall. Slowly Sylvia went up to her and invited her to play with her and her friends.

Resources

(Select one from each category.)

Children's Songbook
- I Pray in Faith (14)
- I Need My Heavenly Father (18)

Hymn
- I Need Thee Every Hour (98)
- More Holiness Give Me (131)

Gospel Art Book
- Young Boy Praying (111)
- Family Prayer (112)

Scriptures
- 3 Nephi 18:15
- D&C 10:5

Sylvia was surprised how quickly her friends accepted the new girl. They didn't seem to care that she was different or wore strange clothing.

That day Sylvia learned that Heavenly Father hears and answers prayers.

Read and discuss 3 Nephi 18:18–20.

+ What does it mean to "watch and pray always"?
+ How does God answer our prayers?

Activity

All Ages: Fill a bowl with candy of different colors (Skittles or M&Ms work well). Have each child take a small handful. For each color of candy, have them name something they can pray for. For example, green might be things we are grateful for, and red might be things we need help with. (Before family home evening begins, make sure you have established a category for each different color of candy.) When everyone has had a turn, reiterate the importance of praying daily. Then eat the candy.

Challenge

This week pray and ask God to help you overcome something you are struggling with.

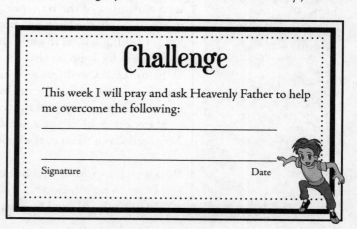

Challenge

This week I will pray and ask Heavenly Father to help me overcome the following:

_____

_____

Signature   Date

Week 2

When I pay my tithing, Heavenly Father will bless me.

Resources

(Select one from each category.)

Children's Songbook
+ I'm Glad to Pay Tithing (150)
+ I Want to Give the Lord My Tenth (150)

Hymn
+ We Give Thee But Thine Own (218)
+ Because I Have Been Given Much (219)

Gospel Art Book
+ Payment of Tithing (113)
+ A Tithe Is a Tenth Part (114)

Scriptures
+ Deuteronomy 14:22
+ D&C 64:23

Lesson

The law of tithing states that we should give one tenth of what we earn to the Lord. Sometimes this seems hard. But when we remember that everything we have comes from God, it is easy to be grateful for the nine-tenths that we get to keep.

To pay tithing, we fill out a donation slip that we get outside of the bishop's office. Then we put the donation slip and our money in an envelope and give it to a member of the bishopric. He makes sure the money is put in the bank and used properly.

Our tithing is used to build churches and temples. It also pays for supplies that we need at church, such as hymn books and lesson manuals. So in reality, the money that we pay for tithing is given back to us because we get to enjoy all the things it is used for.

Many other blessings come from paying tithing. Let's read about them in the book of Malachi.

Read and discuss Malachi 3:8–11.
+ How do we rob God?
+ How are we blessed from paying tithing?

66

Activity

Younger Children: Place ten pennies on a table or another surface where your children can see them. Ask a child to count them. Then ask him how many pennies we should give to Heavenly Father. When your children understand this concept, add more pennies to the table, or use a combination of different coins if your child understands how to count money. Show them how to fill out a tithing envelope if one is available.

Older Children: Make a tithing bank. Decorate a clean, empty cottage cheese container or another disposable container with a lid. Cut a slit in the lid for coins to pass through. When you are finished decorating it, put it in your room or another safe place. Each time you earn some money, determine how much tithing you need to pay and put it in your tithing bank until you can pay it on Sunday.

Challenge

Promise yourself and your Heavenly Father that you will pay tithing each time you earn money.

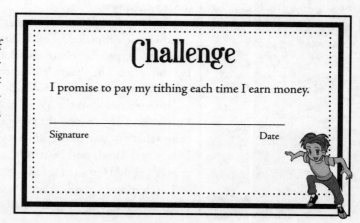

Challenge

I promise to pay my tithing each time I earn money.

_____

Signature   Date

Week 3

I obey the Word of Wisdom by eating and drinking that which is good.

Resources

(Select one from each category.)

Children's Songbook
- The Lord Gave Me a Temple (153)
- The Word of Wisdom (154)

Hymn
- Keep the Commandments (303)
- In Our Lovely Deseret (307)

Gospel Art Book
None

Scriptures
- Proverbs 20:1
- D&C 59:20

Lesson

Have you ever heard that you are the temple of God? That means that your body is like a temple where your spirit dwells. Because your body is so important, you need to take good care of it. To help us care for our bodies, Heavenly Father revealed the Word of Wisdom to Joseph Smith.

The Word of Wisdom states that we should eat healthy foods such as fruit, vegetables, grains, and herbs. Meat is ordained for man, but we should eat it sparingly (only sometimes).

The Word of Wisdom teaches us that we should avoid strong drinks (alcohol), tobacco, and hot drinks. Modern-day prophets have said that hot drinks include tea and coffee. They have also said that taking drugs illegally is against the Word of Wisdom.

We need to follow the Word of Wisdom in order to be healthy. When we eat the proper foods and avoid the things that can hurt us, we will not get sick as often. Our bodies and minds will be strong, and we will have the energy to build God's kingdom.

In addition to good physical health, we will receive other blessings from following the Word of Wisdom.

Let's read about them in Doctrine and Covenants section 89.

Read and discuss 89:18–21.
- What are some of the blessings of following the Word of Wisdom?
- How will the destroying angel pass by us?

Activity

Younger Children: Go into the kitchen and look in the refrigerator and cupboards. Point to all the foods that keep our bodies healthy.

Older Children: Make a healthy snack together, using foods outlined in the Word of Wisdom.

Challenge

It can be hard to eat all our fruits and vegetables. But Heavenly Father has promised great blessings if we do. This week eat the proper number of fruits and vegetables. See if you notice a difference in how your body feels.

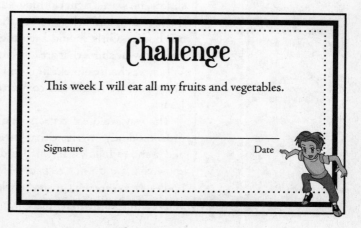

Challenge

This week I will eat all my fruits and vegetables.

_____

Signature   Date

Week 4

When I dress modestly, I respect my body as a gift from God.

Resources

(Select one from each category.)

Children's Songbook
+ The Lord Gave Me a Temple (153)
+ I Have Two Ears (269)

Hymn
+ Dearest Children, God Is Near You (96)
+ As Zion's Youth in Latter-days (256)

Gospel Art Book
+ Young Couple Going to the Temple (120)

Scriptures
+ Genesis 3:21
+ D&C 42:40

Lesson

You've probably heard that we are created in the image of God. That means our bodies are sacred and we need to take good care of them and protect them. Dressing modestly is one way to show respect for our bodies and recognize that they are a gift from God.

Modern-day prophets have taught us what it means to dress modestly. In the pamphlet "For the Strength of Youth," we are taught that we should not wear short shorts and skirts, tight clothing, shirts that do not cover the stomach, and other clothes that show too much of our bodies. Girls should keep their shoulders covered and not wear shirts that are low-cut in the front or back. When we choose our clothing and hairstyles, we should make sure we would feel comfortable if we were with Jesus.

The way we dress reflects who we are inside. If we dress modestly, we show that we love Heavenly Father and want to follow Him. If we dress immodestly, we show that we do not respect Heavenly Father or our bodies. If you are not sure if your clothes are modest, ask your parents or Primary teacher for help.

Read and discuss 1 Timothy 2:9.

- How can we dress modestly?
- Why does Heavenly Father want us to dress modestly?

Activity

Younger Children: See page 72.
Older Children: Have a fashion show featuring modest clothing.

Challenge

Go through all your clothes and set aside anything that is immodest. Discuss with your parents if there is anything you can do to make the clothes modest. If not, get rid of them.

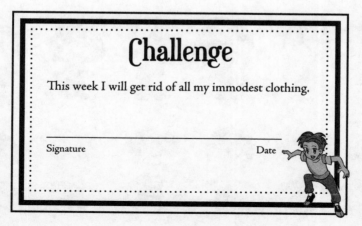

Challenge

This week I will get rid of all my immodest clothing.

_____

Signature   Date

Dressing Modestly Shows Respect

Circle the children who are dressed modestly and are showing respect for their bodies.

July

I Choose the Right by Living Gospel Principles

Wherefore, let us be faithful in keeping the commandments of the Lord

(1 Nephi 3:16).

Week 1

Fasting and prayer can strengthen my testimony.

Resources

(Select one from each category.)

Children's Songbook
+ A Prayer Song (22)
+ We Bow Our Heads (25)

Hymn
+ Bless Our Fast, We Pray (138)
+ In Fasting We Approach Thee (139)

Gospel Art Book
+ Young Boy Praying (111)
+ Family Prayer (112)

Scriptures
+ Psalm 35:13
+ Alma 45:1

Lesson

On the first Sunday of each month, we have fast and testimony during sacrament meeting. Have you ever born your testimony in sacrament meeting? How did you feel? Sharing your testimony is a great way to strengthen it. Fasting is another way.

When we fast, we usually skip two meals. Going without food helps us control our bodies, which helps us focus more on our spirits. We can better feel the influence of the Holy Ghost and His promptings.

You can fast for many different things: to gain a testimony, to better understand the scriptures, for help with a problem, for healing for yourself or another person, and the list goes on and on. Whatever you fast for, if you are sincere, your testimony of Jesus Christ will grow as you see Heavenly Father answering your prayers.

Read and discuss Alma 5:46.

+ What did Alma do to gain a testimony?
+ How can fasting and prayer strengthen our testimonies?

74

Activity

Younger Children: Color the picture on page 76.
Older Children: See page 77.

Challenge

Next fast Sunday make a special effort to fast. If you are not able to fast for the full twenty-four hours, fast for just part of the day. Or give up something you usually eat but can go without (such as candy).

Challenge

I will make a special effort to fast next fast Sunday.

_____   _____
Signature   Date

Fasting Strengthens My Testimony

Secret Code

Using the key below, decode the message. *Solution on page 140.*

A = ✪	H = ✦	O = ➡	V = ✧
B = ◗	I = ◙	P = ◀	W = ♥
C = ☆	J = ✩	Q = ♡	X = O
D = ▢	K = ✫	R = ◚	Y = ◉
E = ★	L = ✺	S = ♥	Z = ✬
F = ✦	M = ⇨	T = ▶	
G = ✱	N = ⇦	U = ◀	

Week 2

Being kind is doing and saying nice things to others.

Resources

(Select one from each category.)

Children's Songbook
+ Kindness Begins with Me (145)
+ We Are Different (263)

Hymn
+ Let Us Oft Speak Kind Words (232)
+ Each Life That Touches Ours for Good (293)

Gospel Art Book
+ Service (115)

Scriptures
+ Galatians 5:13
+ Mosiah 4:15

Lesson

"Jesus said love everyone. Treat them kindly too. When your heart is filled with love, others will love you."

You've probably heard or sung that song recently. But have you done what it says to do? Have you been kind to others? Jesus taught that the first and greatest commandment is to love God. The second is to "love thy neighbor as thyself" (Matthew 22:39).

One of the ways we can show love and kindness to others is saying nice things to them. We can tell them that we appreciate them, that they look nice, or that we admire their talents.

But being kind is much more than just saying nice things. We must also show kindness in our actions. Did you know that if you smile at someone he might be happier the rest of the day? Or that if you help your mom prepare dinner she will know that you love her?

Our words and actions teach people who we really are. If we are kind to others, they will know that we want to follow Jesus Christ.

78

Read and discuss 1 Corinthians 13:4.

+ What is charity?
+ How does it make us kind?

Activity

All Ages: Take turns saying something nice about each family member. One of the parents starts by throwing a ball or another soft object to one of the children. Each family member says something kind about that person. Then the child who received the compliments throws the ball to another family member. Continue this pattern until everyone has received compliments.

Challenge

Be kind to your siblings this week. Each time you are tempted to say an unkind word, stop yourself and say something kind instead.

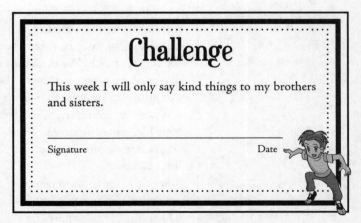

Challenge

This week I will only say kind things to my brothers and sisters.

_____

Signature   Date

Week 3

Reverence is deep respect and love toward God.

Resources

(Select one from each category.)

Children's Songbook
- Reverently, Quietly (26)
- I Want to Be Reverent (28)

Hymn
- Oh, May My Soul Commune with Thee (123)
- Reverently and Meekly Now (185)

Gospel Art Book
None

Scriptures
- Psalm 89:7
- Hebrews 12:28

Lesson

You've probably heard the word *reverence* a lot at church. But do you know what it means? To be reverent means to show love and respect toward God. We go to church to worship God, so it's important to be reverent and show Him that you are listening to the lessons and talks.

What are some of the ways we can be reverent? We can go to church on time so we don't disrupt the meeting when others are trying to be reverent. We can sit quietly and fold our arms so we won't be tempted to play with things we shouldn't at church. We can close our mouths and open our ears. We can raise our hands when we have a question or comment and wait for the teacher to call on us.

When we are reverent, we are able to learn more about Heavenly Father and Jesus. We also help others learn better because we create a place where the Holy Ghost can dwell.

Another way to show reverence and respect for God is to honor His name. We should speak of Him kindly and never take His name in vain.

Read and discuss Doctrine and Covenants 107:4.

- How was naming the priesthood after Melchizedek showing reverence and respect toward God?
- What else can we do to show reverence and respect toward God?

Activity

All Ages: Listen to some hymns or Primary songs together. Practice sitting quietly and thinking about the words to the music. Ask your children what they thought about while the music played. Explain how listening to the prelude music before church meetings can help us get in the right mindset and be reverent.

Challenge

Next Sunday go to church early. Sit reverently and listen to the prelude music. Think about Jesus and how you can set an example to others to be reverent.

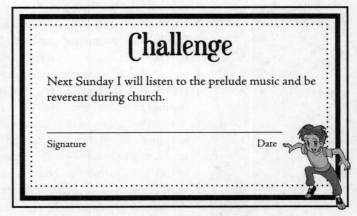

Challenge

Next Sunday I will listen to the prelude music and be reverent during church.

_____

Signature   Date

Week 4

Honesty is telling the truth regardless of the consequences.

Lesson

One day Carl's teacher excitedly told the class that Carl was the only one who scored 100 percent on a test. She said she was very proud of him and would give him a treat after school.

Carl felt sick to his stomach. He knew he had cheated and didn't deserve the praise—or the reward. The end of the day couldn't come soon enough. Carl wanted to run out the door and run home to his room and hide. He remembered lessons he'd had at church and in family home evening about being honest. He knew he had not been honest when he cheated on the test.

For a brief moment, Carl felt a spark of hope when he realized that he could repent. But then he felt sad again because he didn't want to tell his teacher he had cheated.

Finally, Carl decided to be honest and confess what he had done. When the teacher called him to her desk after school to give him his reward, he told her what had happened. His teacher said she was very disappointed and would have to give him a 0 on the test. She said that was the rule in her classroom. Carl was very sad but knew it was more important to be honest than to get a good grade. When he said his bedtime prayer that night, he felt a peaceful feeling overcome him. He knew that he had done the right thing and that Heavenly Father was pleased with him. It didn't matter if he had failed the test because he had been honest.

Read and discuss Doctrine and Covenants 10:28.
+ What happens when we are not honest?
+ How are we blessed when we are honest?

Activity

Younger Children: Tell your children two things that are true and one thing that isn't. For example, "I am wearing blue pants (true), the sky is purple (not true), and you are ___ years old (true)." Ask the children which of your statements was not true. Help them understand what it means to be honest. Use more true/untrue statements if necessary.

Older Children:
See page 84.

Challenge

Be honest at all times this week, even if you know you might get in trouble.

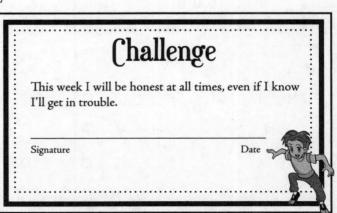

Challenge

This week I will be honest at all times, even if I know I'll get in trouble.

_____

Signature   Date

Missing Vowels

THIRTEENTH ARTICLE OF FAITH

Below is part of the thirteenth article of faith. Fill in all the missing vowels to discover what it says about honesty. *Solution on page 140.*

> Do you know the entire thirteenth article of faith?

```
        A A A
  E E E E E E E E E E E
      I I I I I I
    O O O O O O
      U U U
```

W__   B__L__ __V__   __N   B__ __NG

H__N__ST,   TR__ __,   CH__ST__,

B__ N__ V__ L__ NT,   V__ RT__ __ __ S,

__ND   __N   D__ __NG   G__ __D   T__

__LL   M__N.

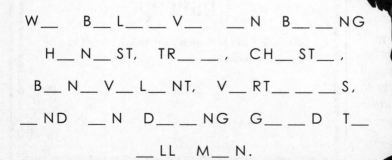

84

August

I Choose to Fill My Life with Things That Invite the Spirit

If there is anything virtuous, lovely, or of good report or praiseworthy, we seek after these things (Articles of Faith 1:13).

Week 1

Having good friends will help me choose the right.

Resources

(Select one from each category.)

Children's Songbook
+ Come with Me to Primary (255)
+ Friends Are Fun (262)

Hymn
+ You Can Make the Pathway Bright (228)
+ Each Life that Touches Ours for Good (293)

Gospel Art Book
+ Living Water (36)
+ Christ in the Home of Mary and Martha (45)

Scriptures
+ Proverbs 14:20
+ James 4:4

Lesson

Who is your best friend? Does he or she help you choose the right, or does he or she encourage you to do things you know you shouldn't?

Imagine if Jesus were your best friend. He would stand beside you each day and lovingly help you choose the right. If you were about to make a wrong choice, He would help you choose something better.

It can be hard to choose the right, but having good friends can make it easy. If we surround ourselves with good friends, they will be an example to us. They will support us when we stand up for what's right and encourage us to do what's right when we struggle.

Read and discuss Proverbs 27:17.s
+ How does "a man sharpeneth the countenance of his friend"?
+ How can you be a good friend?

Activity

Younger Children: Print the picture on page 88. Make enough copies for each child. Tell your children you are going to tell them about several different children. Instruct them to hold up the picture if the child you describe sounds like a good friend who will help them choose the right. **Examples:** 1) Kara asks me to read the scriptures with her. 2) You and Mark are at the candy store. He tells you no one will notice if you steal a sucker. He says he does it all the time. 3) Brian invites the new child in the class to play with your group of friends. 4) Sara tries to convince you to go to the movies on Sunday, even though she knows you're trying to honor the Sabbath day. 5) Caleb turns off the TV when an inappropriate commercial comes on. 6) Rebecca suggests the two of you help her neighbor rake the leaves in his yard.

Older Children: See page 89. In the space provided, write five traits that make a good friend.

Challenge

With your parents' permission, invite one of your friends over to play this week, or to a family activity. Play a wholesome game or do another activity that Jesus would approve of.

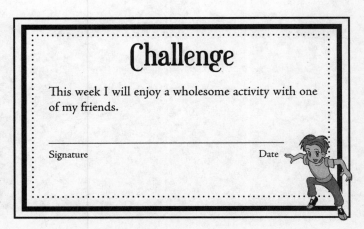

Challenge

This week I will enjoy a wholesome activity with one of my friends.

_____

Signature   Date

A Good Friend Is:

1.

2.

3.

4.

5.

Week 2

I should read, listen to, and look at things pleasing to Heavenly Father.

Resources

(Select one from each category.)

Children's Songbook
- Hum Your Favorite Hymn (152)
- Our Primary Colors (258)

Hymn
- Do What Is Right (237)
- Teach Me to Walk in the Light (304)

Gospel Art Book
None

Scriptures
- Romans 12:1–2
- 2 Corinthians 3:16

Lesson

God gave us the Word of Wisdom to help us understand how to take care of our bodies. Because of the Word of Wisdom, we know what substances can harm our bodies. Just as we shouldn't put harmful things into our bodies, we shouldn't put harmful things into our minds.

The prophets have taught that we should read, listen to, and look at things that are pleasing to Heavenly Father. Sometimes we read books or listen to music that make us feel bad. They say things that are contrary to Jesus's teachings and chase the Holy Ghost away. Sometimes we see images in magazines or on TV that show people wearing immodest clothing or doing other things that are against the commandments. We should not look at these things because they can put bad thoughts in our minds and lead us to temptation. It seems like bad images are everywhere, and sometimes we see them even though we don't want to. When that happens, the best thing to do is to immediately look away and think about something good. We can say a prayer, sing a hymn or

Primary song, or think about Jesus. As we do these things, we will be protected from the evil influences around us.

Read and discuss Mosiah 2:37.

- What things make our bodies unholy?
- What things can we read or listen to that will make our bodies holy?

Activity

All Ages: Read, listen to, or watch something with a good message. It doesn't have to be a Church-made product, but it should be clean and inspiring. Discuss with your children how the story, song, or movie made them feel and what they learned from it. Reiterate the importance of choosing our entertainment carefully.

Challenge

This week read, watch, and listen to only wholesome things. If you start something and don't feel that the Savior would approve, stop immediately and find something else to do.

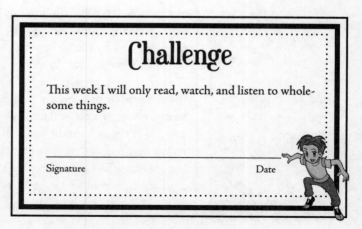

Challenge

This week I will only read, watch, and listen to wholesome things.

_____   _____
Signature   Date

Weeks 3 & 4

I should honor the Sabbath day.

Lesson

Heavenly Father has set apart the Sabbath day (Sunday) as a day of rest and a time when we can focus on worshipping. The most important thing we can do on the Sabbath day is attend all our church meetings and partake of the sacrament. But after we come home from church, we should still focus our thoughts on Heavenly Father.

Many of the activities we do during the week are not appropriate to do on Sunday. For example, if possible, parents should not go to work. We shouldn't shop or go to movies or sporting events.

Instead, we should do things that help us grow in the gospel or grow together as a family. We can read the scriptures or Church magazines, visit the sick, write in our journals, call family members who live far away, visit the sick, or do family history.

We may feel like we have to give up a lot on Sunday, but Heavenly Father will bless us if we keep the Sabbath day holy. Let's read about some of those blessings.

Read and discuss D&C 59:9–19.

- ◆ How can we keep the Sabbath day holy?
- ◆ What blessings will we receive for honoring the Sabbath day?

Activity

Younger Children: See page 94.

Older Children: Assign each family member a number from 1 to 6. (If you have more than six people in your family, you can create teams of 2.) Roll a die. The person who has been assigned the number displayed on the die names something we can do to honor the Sabbath. Repeat until everyone has had a turn.

Challenge

The prophets haven't outlined everything we should and shouldn't do on the Sabbath. Some of it is up to us to decide. As a family, discuss what activities are appropriate to do on the Sabbath. Will you watch TV? Do homework? Then commit to abide by these rules and keep the Sabbath day holy.

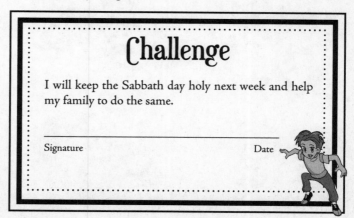

Challenge

I will keep the Sabbath day holy next week and help my family to do the same.

_____

Signature   Date

The Sabbath Day

Put a giant X on the pictures that show things we shouldn't do on the Sabbath day.

1

4

7

2

5

3

6

1. Go to church
2. Go to school
3. Write in your journal
4. Spend time with family
5. Go camping
6. Visit the sick
7. Play sports

September

The Ten Commandments Teach Me to Love God and His Children

If thou lovest me thou shalt serve me and keep all my commandments
(D&C 42:29).

Week 1

We are blessed when we keep the commandments.

Lesson

When Nephi and his family were searching for the promised land, the Lord told them, "Inasmuch as ye shall keep my commandments ye shall prosper in the land; but inasmuch as ye will not keep my commandments ye shall be cut off from my presence" (2 Nephi 1:20). The same promise applies to each of us. When we obey the commandments, Heavenly Father will bless us.

[Explain to your children some of the blessings you have received for keeping the commandments. Be as specific as possible and use terms they can understand. Then ask them how they have been blessed by keeping the commandments.]

Read and discuss Doctrine and Covenants 82:10.
+ Why is the Lord bound when we do what He says?
+ What does it mean to "have no promise"?

96

Activity

All Ages: Organize a commandments treasure hunt for your children, hiding each clue in a place that relates to a commandment. Older children should help the younger ones and help them figure out the clues. Place a treat or another reward at the end of the hunt. Explain to your children the correlation between the treasure hunt and how we are blessed for keeping the commandments.

You can use the following clues or come up with your own:

- No other gods before me (hide the clue near a picture of the Savior)
- Keep the Sabbath day holy (near a calendar or someone's church shoes)
- Honor thy father and mother (in parents' room or on their bed)
- Pay your tithing (near a piggy bank)
- Keep the Word of Wisdom (on the refrigerator)
- Dress modestly (in someone's closet or dresser)

Challenge

Think about which commandments you need to do better at following. Pick one of them and try to obey it all week.

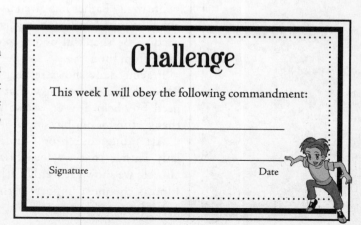

Challenge

This week I will obey the following commandment:

_____

_____

Signature   Date

Week 2

I should respect and worship God.

Resources

(Select one from each category.)

Children's Songbook
+ God's Love (97)
+ Because God Loves Me (234)

Hymn
+ With Songs of Praise (71)
+ How Great Thou Art (86)

Gospel Art Book
+ Boy Praying (115)

Scriptures
+ Psalm 99:5
+ Matthew 4:10

Lesson

Jesus taught, "Thou shalt love the Lord thy God with all thy heart, and with all thy soul, and with all thy mind. This is the first and great commandment" (Matthew 22:37). Jesus showed His love and respect for Heavenly Father by keeping the commandments and serving others. When we follow Jesus's example, we also show our love and respect to Heavenly Father.

Heavenly Father has given us everything we have: our lives, our families, our friends, our homes. We need to be thankful and recognize that all things come from Him.

Praying daily shows respect to Heavenly Father. Through prayer we show that we are humble and need His help. Prayer is also a time when we can thank Him for our blessings.

Attending church on Sunday also shows Heavenly Father that we love Him. When we go to church, we show Heavenly Father that worshipping Him is the most important thing we can do with our time.

Heavenly Father is always pouring out blessings upon us. We need to show Him that we are grateful and that we love Him in return.

Read and discuss Mosiah 2:20–21.

+ How has Heavenly Father blessed us?
+ What is an unprofitable servant? Why did King Benjamin say we are unprofitable servants?

Activity

Younger Children: Go on a picture scavenger hunt. Look through magazines or books and find five pictures that show people respecting God or His creations.

Older Children: Go on a scripture scavenger hunt. Find five scriptures that talk about respecting or worshiping God.

Challenge

Praying daily is one of the ways we show respect to Heavenly Father. Make a special effort this week to thank Him for blessings that you sometimes take for granted.

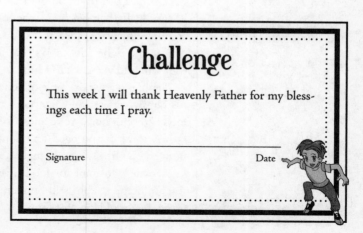

Challenge

This week I will thank Heavenly Father for my blessings each time I pray.

_____   _____
Signature   Date

I should honor my parents.

Resources

(Select one from each category.)

Children's Songbook
+ Love Is Spoken Here (190)
+ The Family (194)

Hymn
+ Love at Home (294)
+ Home Can Be a Heaven on Earth (298)

Gospel Art Book
+ Family Prayer (112)

Scriptures
+ Exodus 20:12
+ Colossians 3:20

Lesson

Just as Heavenly Father loves all of His children, your parents love you and want the best for you. They ask you to behave a certain way or do certain things because they want you to follow Jesus Christ. They know that if you follow Jesus Christ, you will be happy.

The fifth commandment states, "Honour thy father and thy mother: that thy days may be long upon the land which the Lord thy God giveth thee" (Exodus 20:12). Heavenly Father has made honoring your parents a commandment because He knows they can help you choose the right. He knows that if they are righteous, they will lead you back to Him.

Nephi is a good example of honoring parents. When his family was in the wilderness, they were in need of food. Nephi's bow broke and his family, including his father, were discouraged and complained about their hunger. Nephi was able to make a new bow but did not know where to hunt for food. Even though his father was unhappy, Nephi still honored him by asking him where he should look for food.

Read and discuss 1 Nephi 16:18–23.

+ Why did Nephi ask his father where to hunt for food?
+ How can you honor your parents?

Activity

All Ages: Draw a picture of you and your parents doing something all of you love. Hang it in your room as a reminder to honor and obey your parents.

Challenge

Make a special effort to honor your parents this week. Do not complain when they ask you to do your chores or go to bed. Tell them how much you love them and find ways you can help them without being asked.

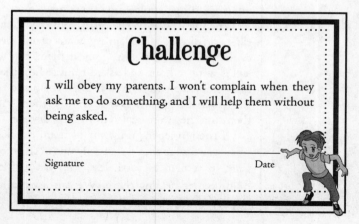

Challenge

I will obey my parents. I won't complain when they ask me to do something, and I will help them without being asked.

_____

Signature   Date

Week 4

I should respect others.

Resources

(Select one from each category.)

Children's Songbook
+ Jesus Said Love Everyone (61)
+ We Are Different (263)

Hymn
+ Let Us Oft Speak Kind Words (232)
+ Love One Another (308)

Gospel Art Book
None

Scriptures
+ Philippians 2:3
+ D&C 38:24–25

Lesson

We are all created differently. Some people have dark hair, while others have light hair. Some people are tall, some people are short, and some people are in between. In addition, some people go to church and believe in Jesus Christ, while other people do not. No matter how different we may be, Heavenly Father has taught us to respect each other. We may not have the same interests or beliefs as others, but that doesn't mean we can't be kind. Jesus taught us to love everyone, including people who others may shun.

When Jesus was on the earth, some people had a terrible skin disease called leprosy. Many people were afraid of the lepers and wouldn't go near them. But when ten lepers went to Jesus and asked Him to heal them, Jesus had compassion on them. He loved them and respected them even though others were afraid of them. He blessed them and they were healed from their disease.

Of the ten lepers, only one of them thanked Jesus. Jesus was disappointed that only one of them respected Him in return. Nevertheless, He was still kind and didn't regret healing them. We can learn a lot about respecting others from Jesus Christ.

Read and discuss Mosiah 27:3–4.

- What does it mean to esteem our neighbor as yourself?
- How can you show respect to those who are different from you?

Activity

Younger Children: Color the picture on page 104.
Older Children: Learn about another culture. Play a game, eat some food, or read a story from another culture. Discuss how it is similar to and different from what you're used to. How can you respect others?

Challenge

Choose one person you want to do better at respecting this week and make a special effort all week to respect that person. It could be a teacher who you don't always listen to, a child at school who you normally don't play with, or anyone else.

Challenge

This week I will make a special effort to respect the following person:

_____

_____
Signature   Date

I Will Respect Others

October

Blessings of the Priesthood
Are Available to All

And also all they who receive this priesthood
receive me, saith the Lord

(D&C 84:35).

Worthy young men receive the priesthood when they are 12 years old.

Resources

(Select one from each category.)

Children's Songbook
- The Priesthood Is Restored (89)
- A Young Man Prepared (166)

Hymn
- Come, All Ye Sons of God (322)
- See the Mighty Priesthood Gathered (325)

Gospel Art Book
- Ordination to the Priesthood (106)

Scriptures
- D&C 84:111
- D&C 107:85

Lesson

Turning twelve is an exciting time for a boy. Not only does he graduate from Primary, but he also receives the priesthood if he is worthy.

The priesthood is the power and authority God gives to men to direct His church. We need the priesthood to perform ordinances like the sacrament, baptism, and temple ordinances. A man can receive the priesthood if he is a member of the Church, keeps the commandments, and is a certain age. There are different offices in the priesthood, and each office has different responsibilities. For example, when a boy turns twelve, he is ordained to the office of a deacon. He can pass the sacrament, serve as an usher, collect fast offerings, and act as a messenger for another priesthood leader, such as a bishop. He cannot perform other duties, such as baptizing someone, until he is older and ordained to the office of a priest.

Read and discuss Doctrine and Covenants 20:57–59.
- What is the duty of a deacon?
- How can young men prepare to receive the priesthood?

Activity

Younger Children: Color the picture on page 108.

Older Children: Color the picture of the church on page 109. Cut it out and cut along each line so that each office of the priesthood is a separate piece. See if you can put the puzzle back together. Where does a deacon fit into this puzzle? .

Challenge

Young men have to be worthy to receive the priesthood. What can you do now to prepare for it? Choose one trait and work on developing it this week. (Girls can work on a trait such as faith that will help them accept the ordinances of the priesthood.)

Challenge

This week I will work on developing the following trait:

_____

_____
Signature   Date

A Deacon Holds Some of the Keys of the Priesthood

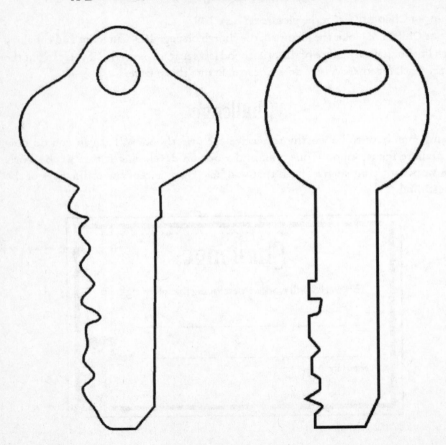

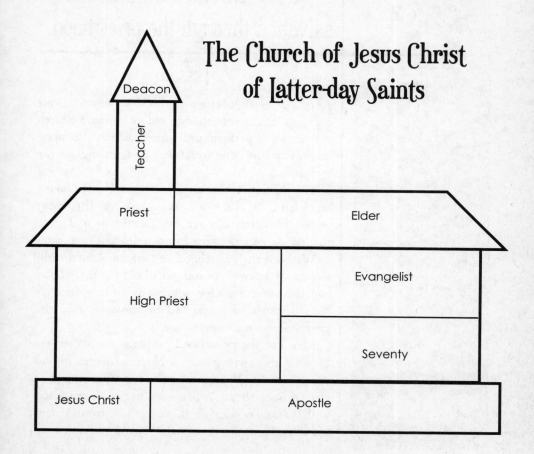

The Church of Jesus Christ of Latter-day Saints

Deacon

Teacher

Priest

Elder

High Priest

Evangelist

Seventy

Jesus Christ

Apostle

Week 2

We receive the ordinances of salvation through the priesthood.

Resources

(Select one from each category.)

Children's Songbook
+ The Priesthood Is Restored (89)
+ The Fifth Article of Faith (125)

Hymn
+ Praise to the Man (27)
+ Hark, All Ye Nations (264)

Gospel Art Book
+ Young Man Being Baptized (103)
+ Salt Lake Temple (119)

Scriptures
+ 3 Nephi 11:21
+ D&C 68:8

Lesson

God has given us the priesthood so we can direct His church. Priesthood holders conduct church meetings and perform ordinances such as the sacrament, baptisms, confirmations, and sealings in the temple.

Worthy males receive the priesthood by the laying on of hands of other priesthood holders. They must be members of the Church, be a certain age, and prove that they are keeping the commandments.

We need the priesthood to perform sacred ordinances. If a person who doesn't hold the priesthood baptizes someone, God will not recognize the baptism. It must be performed by someone with the proper authority, or priesthood.

Men use the priesthood properly when they are blessing and serving others. Having the priesthood does not mean they can force their families or anyone else to obey them. When they use the priesthood with love and gentleness, they and those around them are able to grow in the gospel.

Read and discuss Doctrine and Covenants 107:8.

- ✦ What is priesthood authority?
- ✦ How does the priesthood help us receive ordinances of salvation?

Activity

All Ages: Think of a priesthood holder who has influenced your life (your bishop, grandfather, father, brother, uncle, or cousin). Write him a letter (or draw a picture) and thank him for being worthy to hold the priesthood and for blessing others.

Challenge

With your family, learn about the differences between the Aaronic and Melchizedek priesthoods. Next week during family home evening, see if you can remember three duties of each priesthood.

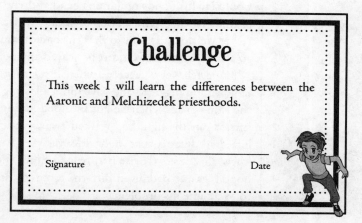

Challenge

This week I will learn the differences between the Aaronic and Melchizedek priesthoods.

_____

Signature   Date

Week 3

I can receive strengthening power through priesthood blessings.

Lesson

There once was a boy named Jamie who was afraid to go to sleep at night. Each night he had scary dreams and woke up crying. It was hard to go back to sleep because he was so scared. Even though he knew his parents were just down the hall, he still feared that something bad would happen to him.

One night Jamie's father explained to him that he was going to give Jamie a priesthood blessing. He would lay his hands on Jamie's head and say a special prayer. Through the power of Jesus Christ, Jamie's father would bless him so that the bad dreams would go away and Jamie wouldn't be scared anymore.

Jamie felt very peaceful when his father laid his hands upon his head and gave him a blessing. He felt the same peace when he got into bed and his father turned out the light and walked away. Jamie did not have bad dreams that night. He was very happy and knew that Jesus Christ had helped him. The priesthood blessing had given him the strength he needed to overcome his problem.

112

Read and discuss Mark 6:5.

+ How did Jesus heal people?
+ How can we be healed today? Can we only have blessings when we are sick?

Activity

All Ages: Watch the video "Sanctify Yourselves" available at https://lds.org/youth/video/sanctify-yourselves?lang=eng

Challenge

Think of a time when you received a priesthood blessing. Write about it in your journal (younger children can have help from their parents). Record as many details as possible, such as how old you were, why you received a blessing, who gave you the blessing, how you felt, and what happened after you received the blessing.

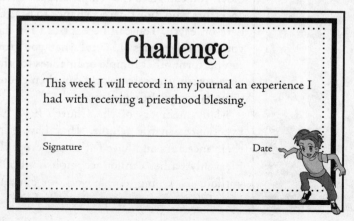

Challenge

This week I will record in my journal an experience I had with receiving a priesthood blessing.

_____

Signature   Date

I can go to the temple for my ancestors when I am older.

Resources

(Select one from each category.)

Children's Songbook
- Family History—I Am Doing It (94)
- Families Can Be Together Forever (188)

Hymn
- High on the Mountain Top (5)
- We Love Thy House, O God (247)

Gospel Art Book
- The Nauvoo Temple (118)
- Temple Baptismal Font (121)

Scriptures
- Matthew 16:19
- 1 Peter 3:19

Lesson

Heavenly Father has commanded all of us to receive the ordinances of the temple in order to return to Him. We need to be baptized, receive our endowment, and be sealed to our spouse. Would it be fair if someone never had a chance to accept these ordinances? Of course not.

Heavenly Father loves us and wants everyone to have a chance to accept the gospel. When you are older, you can go to the temple and do work for your ancestors who didn't have a chance to hear the gospel here on earth. You can be baptized for them when you are twelve years old. And when you grow up, you can perform other temple ordinances for them. Your ancestors in the spirit world can then choose if they want to accept the ordinances.

Many members of the Church have had sacred experiences in the temple. They have felt close to their ancestors and have felt them accept the gospel. Heavenly Father cannot accomplish all of His work without us. Doing temple work for our ancestors is one of the greatest ways we can help Him.

Read and discuss Hebrews 11:40.

+ Why can't our ancestors be made perfect without us?
+ Do you think we need them to be made perfect?

Activity

All Ages: Complete the family tree on page 116.

Challenge

If you live near a temple, visit it as a family. Walk the grounds and discuss the importance of going to the temple when we're older. If the temple has a visitors center, watch a film or look at the various displays that explain temple work.

Challenge

I will visit a temple with my family.

_____

Signature   Date

My Family Tree

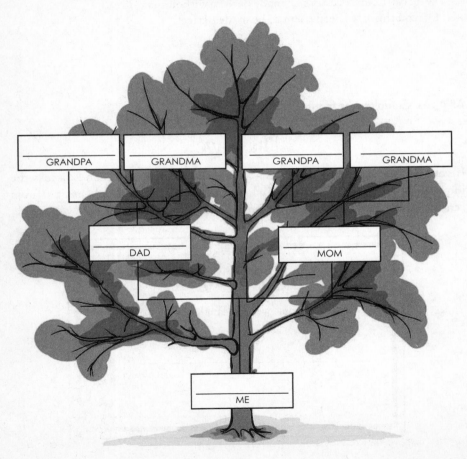

GRANDPA · GRANDMA · GRANDPA · GRANDMA

DAD · MOM

ME

November

I Can Choose to Be
a Missionary Now

*And he said unto them, Go ye into all
the world, and preach the gospel to every creature*
(Mark 16:15).

I can be a missionary by serving others.

Resources

(Select one from each category.)

Children's Songbook
+ Can a Little Child Like Me? (9)
+ When We're Helping (198)

Hymn
+ Have I Done Any Good? (223)
+ Go Forth with Faith (263)

Gospel Art Book
+ Service (115)

Scriptures
+ Mosiah 2:17
+ Alma 34:29

Lesson

Jesus Christ spent His life serving others. Because He was sincere and showed His love to people, they trusted Him and knew that what He taught was true.

If Jesus was on the earth today, He would continue serving others. But since He is not here, we need to help Him serve others.

Serving others is a form of missionary work. Even if we are not talking about the Church, we are speaking loudly with our actions. Our kind acts show others that Jesus loves them. They show that there is much good in the world. They teach that we are all children of God and need to help each other.

When we serve others, we grow closer to Jesus Christ because we are following Him.

Read and discuss Matthew 25:40.
+ How do we serve others when we serve Jesus?
+ Who have you served recently?

Activity

All Ages: Do a service project for a neighbor who is not of our faith.

Challenge

Do a secret act of service for someone this week. You could do a sibling's chores, write someone a kind letter and sign it "From Someone Who Appreciates You" or something similar.

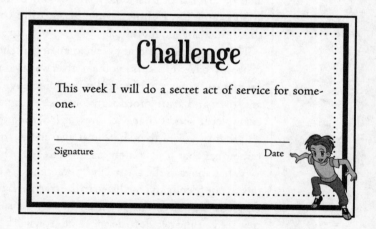

Challenge

This week I will do a secret act of service for someone.

_____
Signature   Date

Week 2

I can be a missionary by setting a good example.

Lesson

Last week we talked about how our kind acts can be a form of missionary work. Other actions can also be a form of missionary work. When we set a good example, we show people how to live the way that Jesus Christ taught.

Have you and a friend ever had an argument? You probably have. How did you act afterward? Did you say you were sorry? Hopefully you did. Saying you are sorry and asking for forgiveness is setting a good example. It shows that you know it is wrong to fight and that you want to do better. It also shows that you remember that Jesus taught us to love each other.

What about in the classroom? Sometimes it's easy to talk to our friends and not listen to the teacher. But if you decide to sit quietly and listen to the teacher, someone may see you and decide to do the same. You will be showing your classmates that it's important to respect others.

We don't always have to use words to teach someone about Jesus. When we set a good example, we show others how to follow Him.

Read and discuss Matthew 5:16.

+ What does it mean to "let your light so shine before men"?
+ How can you be a good example to others?

Activity

Younger Children: Look at the picture on page 122. Answer the following questions with your parents: Who is being a good example? What do you think these boys are talking about? Should these boys be nice to each other even though they're different?

Older Children: Use the space on page 123 to write a story about what is happening in the picture on page 122. If you need help coming up with ideas, refer to the questions above in the Younger Children section.

Challenge

Practice being a good example this week. Try not to get upset with your friends or family. If the kids at school or Primary are being noisy and not listening to the teacher, set a good example by folding your arms and listening.

Challenge

I will be a good example this week.

_____

Signature   Date

I can be a missionary by setting a good example.

Week 3

I can teach my friends about Jesus Christ and His Church.

Resources

(Select one from each category.)

Children's Songbook
- I Want to Be a Missionary Now (168)
- We'll Bring the World His Truth (172)

Hymn
- Hark, All Ye Nations! (264)
- The Time Is Far Spent (266)

Gospel Art Book
- Missionaries: Elders (109)

Scriptures
- Mark 16:15
- D&C 88:81

Lesson

What do you like about going to your friends' houses? Do they have toys and games that you don't have? How do you feel when they share something special with you?

One thing you have that your friends may not is a testimony of Jesus Christ. A testimony of Jesus Christ is the best thing a person can have—even better than an exciting toy, a fancy dress, or a swimming pool. Jesus hopes that all of us who know Him will teach others about Him and His Church. He loves each of us very much and wants us to return to Him.

But He needs our help. He needs us to share our testimonies with our friends and invite them to church with us. He wants us to help them feel how much He loves them.

It can be scary to talk to our friends about Jesus. But Jesus has promised that He will help us have the courage to do it and know what to say.

Read and discuss Doctrine and Covenants 84:85.
- Why shouldn't we worry about what we will say?
- How can we prepare ourselves to share the gospel?

Activity

All Ages: Write letters or draw pictures to send to a missionary. Tell him about your family home evening lesson this week and what you are doing to be a member missionary.

Challenge

Invite one of your nonmember friends to Primary. Or, if that isn't possible, invite him or her to join your family for family home evening or another activity

Challenge

I will invite _____
to Primary.

_____
Signature   Date

I can prepare now to serve a full-time mission.

Resources

(Select one from each category.)

Children's Songbook
- I Hope They Call Me on a Mission (169)
- Called to Serve (174)

Hymn
- The Time Is Far Spent (266)
- I'll Go Where You Want Me to Go (270)

Gospel Art Book
- Missionaries: Sisters (110)

Scriptures
- D&C 4
- D&C 33:8

Lesson

This month we have talked about ways we can do missionary work without serving a mission. We can serve others, we can be a good example, and we can talk to our friends about Jesus Christ. Doing all these things helps us prepare to serve a full-time mission. If we do all these things before we serve a mission, we will not have to learn how to do them when we serve a full-time mission.

Did you also know that our family does things every day that will help you prepare for a mission? We pray together, read the scriptures, and try our best to choose the right. Getting along with each other and asking each other for forgiveness is one of the ways we can prepare to have a missionary companion.

We can also do things like learning to cook, do laundry, mend clothes, and go grocery shopping. Missionaries have to do all these things by themselves. If they don't know how to do these things before they go, it will be harder to focus on their missionary work.

Serving a full-time mission may be years away, but we can do small thing each day to prepare for it

Read and discuss Doctrine and Covenants 11:20–22.

⁑ What must we do before we declare God's word?

⁑ What can you do to prepare for a mission?

Activity

Younger Children: Print page 128 from the resource CD. Cut out the pictures and place them in a paper bag. Have children take turns pulling a picture from the paper bag. After each child gets a picture, ask if the boy in the picture looks like he is preparing to serve a mission. Why or why not?

Older Children: See page 129.

Challenge

This week help your parents with a task such as cooking or doing laundry. If it seems boring, remind yourself that learning how to do that task is preparing you for a mission.

Challenge

This week I will help my parents with the following task:

_____

_____

Signature   Date

Missionary Maze

Help the young elder find his way through the maze to his mission. ***Solution on page 140.***

December

Jesus Christ Is
the Son of God ·

Behold, I am Jesus Christ, the Son of God.
I am the life and the light of the world
(D&C 11:28).

Week 1

Heavenly Father sent His Son to earth.

Lesson

When Heavenly Father presented the plan of salvation, Jesus Christ agreed to be our Savior. Jesus said He would come to earth and teach us how to return to Heavenly Father. Then He would die for us so we could repent of our sins.

Jesus was born as a baby, just like the rest of us. Let's read about His birth in the New Testament.

Read and discuss the birth of Jesus Christ in Luke 2:1–19.
+ Why did the angel tell the shepherds not to fear?
+ Why was Jesus born in a manger?
+ How do you think Mary felt to be the mother of the Savior?

Activity

All Ages: Make a Christmas card for a friend or relative you don't see often. Write a short letter about what you learned about the Savior's birth in family home evening. Bear your testimony of Jesus Christ.

Challenge

Give a copy of "The Living Christ" to a friend or relative who isn't of our faith. You can purchase copies from the distribution center or download a copy from http://lds.org/library/display/0,4945,90-1-10-1,00.html (click "PDF Version" in the upper right corner).

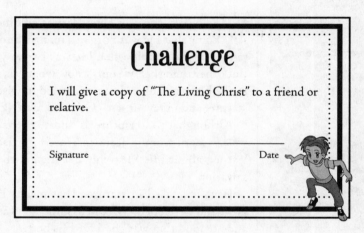

Challenge

I will give a copy of "The Living Christ" to a friend or relative.

_____

Signature   Date

Week 2

Jesus grew in wisdom and stature and in favor with God and man.

Resources

(Select one from each category.)

Children's Songbook
+ Jesus Once Was a Little Child (55)
+ Jesus Loved the Little Children (59)

Hymn
+ Oh, Come, All Ye Faithful (202)
+ Angels We Have Heard on High (203)

Gospel Art Book
+ In Favour with God (33)
+ Christ in the Temple (34)

Lesson

We don't know a lot about Jesus's childhood. We know that He was born in a manger and that He taught in the temple when He was twelve years old. But other than that, we only know what was recorded in the book of Luke: "Jesus increased in wisdom and stature, and in favour with God and man" (2:52).

Although this scripture is short, there is much we can learn from it. Jesus increased in wisdom. He learned about His Heavenly Father and the plan of salvation.

Jesus increased in stature. That means His body grew and developed. We can assume He was healthy and ate food that was good for His body.

Jesus increased in favour with God and man. People loved Him. In the scriptures we can read many examples of His kindness. He obeyed His Father at all times and helped others feel good about themselves.

How was Jesus's childhood like yours? What can you do this week to be more like Him?

Activity

All Ages: As a family bake some cookies or another treat and deliver them to your neighbors. Wish them a merry Christmas.

Challenge

Memorize the Primary song "Jesus Once Was a Little Child." Sing it to yourself when you are tempted to make a wrong choice.

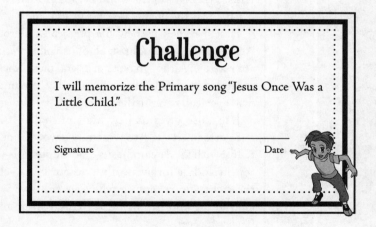

Challenge

I will memorize the Primary song "Jesus Once Was a Little Child."

_____

Signature   Date

Week 3

Jesus Christ is the light and the life of the world.

Lesson

When Jesus Christ appeared to the Nephites, he said, "Behold, I am the light and the life of the world." Jesus is the light of the world because He shows us the truth. He is the life because He gives us new life.

First, he gives us new life physically. Through the Atonement of Jesus Christ, all of us will be resurrected after we die. Although our spirits and our bodies will be separated for a time, they will someday be reunited and made perfect, never to die again.

Jesus also gives us new life spiritually. If He had not performed the Atonement, we would not be able to live with God again. Jesus made it possible for us to repent and be forgiven. If we do our best—choosing the right and repenting when we sin—we will have eternal life and live with Heavenly Father and Jesus Christ forever.

Read and discuss John 14:6.
+ According to this scripture, who is Jesus?
+ How does He help us come unto the Father?

136

Activity

All Ages: Attend a Christmas event centered around Jesus Christ. If there isn't one available in your community, have your own at home. Sing Christmas carols together, act out the Nativity, or do another activity that helps you remember the true meaning of Christmas.

Challenge

Write your testimony in the front cover of a Book of Mormon. Give it to one of your friends or to the full-time missionaries to give to an investigator.

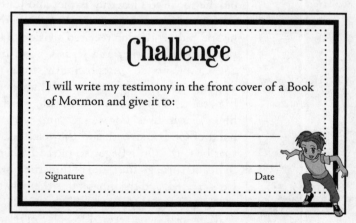

Challenge

I will write my testimony in the front cover of a Book of Mormon and give it to:

_____

_____
Signature   Date

Joseph Smith saw and testified of Jesus Christ.

Lesson

Joseph Smith was a very special prophet. He restored the true Church of Jesus Christ and translated the Book of Mormon. But in addition, he saw and testified of Jesus Christ. When Joseph was fourteen years old, he spoke to Heavenly Father and Jesus Christ in the Sacred Grove. Later, when he became the prophet, he and Sidney Rigdon received a vision of heaven and saw Heavenly Father and Jesus Christ. In Doctrine and Covenants 76, Joseph Smith wrote: "And now, after the many testimonies which have been given of him, this is the testimony, last of all, which we give of him: That he lives! For we saw him, even on the right hand of God; and we heard the voice bearing record that he is the Only Begotten of the Father—That by him, and through him, and of him, the worlds are and were created, and the inhabitants thereof are begotten sons and daughters unto God" (vv. 22–24).

Many people persecuted Joseph Smith for his testimony of Christ. They called him foolish and said that he didn't really see Jesus Christ. But Joseph never denied what he saw. He had a strong testimony and was committed to bringing the truth to the world, even though it meant giving his own life.

In 1844, Joseph Smith was killed in Carthage Jail. It was a very sad time for the members of the Church, but they were comforted by their testimonies of Jesus Christ. Joseph Smith had taught them that death is only temporary. And they knew that because of his faith in Jesus Christ and because he always chose the right, Joseph Smith would find glory in the celestial kingdom.

Read and discuss D&C 135:3.

+ How did Joseph Smith do more, save Jesus only, for the salvation of men than any other man?
+ What does it mean that he lived great and died great?

Activity

All Ages: Watch *The Restoration*, available in the media library at www.lds.org.

Challenge

Next week bear your testimony of the Savior during fast and testimony meeting.

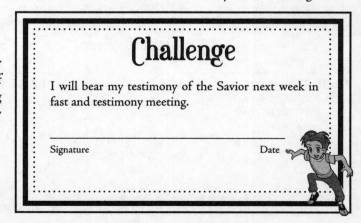

Challenge

I will bear my testimony of the Savior next week in fast and testimony meeting.

_____

Signature   Date

Answer Key

PAGE 8

PAGE 9

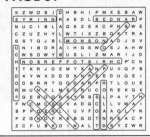

PAGE 31

PAGE 36

PAGE 50

1. ADMIT
2. SORROW
3. FORSAKE
4. CONFESS
5. RESTITUTION
6. FORGIVE
7. OBEY
8. ENDURE TO THE END

PAGE 62

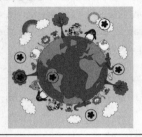

PAGE 77

FASTING AND PRAYER CAN STRENGTHEN MY TESTIMONY.

PAGE 84

WE BELIEVE IN BEING HONEST, TRUE, CHASTE, BENEVEOLENT, VIRTUOUS, AND IN DOING GOOD TO ALL MEN.

PAGE 129

Fun Food for FHE

Simple, Kid-Friendly Recipes

These recipes may not be fancy, but they're simple, fun foods that children of all ages will enjoy making and eating.

Frozen Yogurt Pie

3 (6-oz.) cartons of yogurt
1 (8-oz.) carton whipped topping
1 pre-made graham cracker crust or pie shell

1. Mix together yogurt and whipped topping.

2. Pour mixture into crust.

3. Freeze until hardened.

Vanilla Pudding

¼ c. flour
¾ c. sugar
¼ tsp. salt
2 Tbsp. cornstarch
3 egg yolks
3 cups milk
1 tsp. vanilla

1. In a medium-sized saucepan, combine dry ingredients. Stir in wet ingredients.
2. Cook on medium heat, stirring constantly, until thick.

Variation: For chocolate, add 2½ squares baking chocolate and ¹/₃ cup sugar.

Cake Mix Sandwich Cookies

1 box cake mix of your choice
2 eggs
½ cup vegetable oil
1 small tub vanilla frosting

1. Mix together all ingredients except frosting.

2. Roll dough into little balls. Place on ungreased cookie sheet.

3. Bake at 350 degrees for 8–10 minutes.

4. When cookies are completely cool, make sandwiches by frosting a cookie and placing another one on top.

Five-minute Ice Cream

1 (12-oz.) pkg. frozen strawberries (or other berries of your choice)
²/₃ cup heavy cream
½ cup sugar
1 tsp. vanilla

1. Place all ingredients in a food processor or blender.
2. Blend until mixture resembles ice cream. If mixture appears too thick, add more cream, 1 tablespoon at a time, until desired consistency is reached.

Fudge in a Bag

½ cup cream cheese
1 pound powdered sugar
½ cup baking cocoa
2 Tbsp. butter
2 (1-gal.) Ziplock bags

1. Put all ingredients in one of the bags and seal bag. Place in the remaining bag and seal.

2. Take turns mixing the fudge by squishing the bag. Continue until fudge is smooth and ready to eat (takes 15–30 minutes).

Easy Stovetop S'mores

1 pkg. fudge-striped cookies (or chocolate-covered graham crackers)
1 pkg. marshmallows

1. Place a marshmallow on a chopstick, skewer, or other long, pointy object. (Even the end of a spoon will even work if that's all you have.)
2. Hold marshmallow a few inches away from the stove burner (on medium heat) until marshmallow is "roasted" to your liking.
3. Place marshmallow between two cookies and enjoy!

Chocolate-covered Pretzels

2 cups chocolate chips or chocolate candy pieces
1 Tbsp. vegetable shortening
1 (9-oz.) bag mini pretzels

1. Combine chocolate and shortening in a microwave-safe bowl. Microwave for 1 minute and then stir. Microwave 1 more minute and stir. Repeat until chocolate is melted.

2. Remove chocolate from microwave. Dip pretzels in chocolate, allowing excess chocolate to drip off.

3. Place dipped pretzels on wax paper or a cookie sheet sprayed with cooking spray.

4. Leave pretzels in a cool place until chocolate is hardened.

Fruit Smoothie
Serves 6

    3 cups milk
    1 (8-oz.) carton vanilla yogurt
    6 ice cubes
    1 banana
    3 cups berries of your choice
    Sugar to taste

Combine all ingredients and mix in blender until smooth. If you want a thinner smoothie, add more milk. For a thicker consistency, add more fruit and yogurt.

Variations
Instead of berries, use peaches or mangoes. For a tropical smoothie, substitute pineapple for berries, and use 1 cup coconut milk and 2 cups regular milk.

No Bake Cookies

2 cups sugar
½ cup butter
½ cup baking cocoa
½ cup milk
½ cup peanut butter
1 tsp. vanilla
3 cups quick oats

1. In a saucepan stir together sugar, butter, cocoa, and milk. Bring to a boil for 2 minutes.

2. Add peanut butter, vanilla, and oats.

3. Drop by teaspoon on wax paper. Cookies will harden as they cool.

Other Books by Kimiko Christensen Hammari

I Know the Scriptures Are True
I Know My Savior Lives
The Book of Mormon Puzzle Book
The Doctrine and Covenants Puzzle Book
The Old Testament Puzzle Book
The New Testament Puzzle Book
Teeny Tiny Talks: I'll Follow Him in Faith
Teeny Tiny Talks: I Am a Child of God
Teeny Tiny Talks: My Eternal Family
Christmas Games and Goodies

0 26575 59414 0